The Library Workplace Idea Book

ALA Editions purchases fund advocacy,
awareness, and accreditation programs
for library professionals worldwide.

THE
LIBRARY WORKPLACE
IDEA BOOK

Proactive Steps for Positive Change

Edited by
HEATHER L. SEIBERT,
AMANDA VINOGRADOV,
and AMANDA H. McLELLAN

CHICAGO | 2020

Extensive effort has gone into ensuring the reliability of the information in this book; however, the publisher makes no warranty, express or implied, with respect to the material contained herein.

ISBN: 978-0-8389-4645-9 (paper)

Library of Congress Cataloging-in-Publication Data

Names: Seibert, Heather L., 1975- editor. | Vinogradov, Amanda, 1985- editor. | McLellan, Amanda H., 1982- editor.
Title: The library workplace idea book : proactive steps for positive change / edited by Heather L. Seibert, Amanda Vinogradov, and Amanda H. McLellan.
Description: Chicago : ALA Editions, 2020. | Includes bibliographical references and index. | Summary: "The coeditors of The Library Workplace Idea Book: Proactive Steps for Positive Change have gathered ideas for positive change from library workers at all levels. Case studies and personal narratives will inspire your advocacy and action for a better library workplace"— Provided by publisher.
Identifiers: LCCN 2019041458 | ISBN 9780838946459 (paperback)
Subjects: LCSH: Library personnel management—United States. | Library personnel management—United States—Case studies. | Academic libraries—Personnel management—United States. | Library employees—Attitudes. | Library employees—Psychology. | Quality of work life.
Classification: LCC Z682.2.U5 L545 2020 | DDC 023—dc23
LC record available at https://lccn.loc.gov/2019041458

Cover design by Karen Sheets de Gracia. Interior design by Kim Thornton in the Chapparal and Museo typefaces.

♾ This paper meets the requirements of ANSI/NISO Z39.48-1992 (Permanence of Paper).

Printed in the United States of America

24 23 22 21 20   5 4 3 2 1

For Zoe and Silas—because you matter.

CONTENTS

I n 2012, Amanda V. and I (Heather) discovered that we were pregnant at the same time while both working in the Technical Services Division at Joyner Library, East Carolina University (ECU). It was only after asking for lactation accommodations when returning to work that we both realized how difficult having the needs of the employee met in an institutional setting could be. In a perfect scenario, we would have contacted human resources and the system would have provided us with the accommodations needed. Unfortunately, we faced some unexpected and frustrating barriers. It took many years of advocacy, tears, frustration and (unfortunately) burned bridges for us to bring these shortfalls to light and help to bring about an institutional change that would benefit all lactating mothers on campus.

In the past six years since Amanda and I began our advocacy for change on campus we have spoken at various conferences, met with administrators, gave lightning talks, presented posters, and spoke at a Women and Gender Studies event. Granted, many moments during this time were spent trying to strategize when to interject our advocacy for lactation support into workplace conversations. One observation that we have heard many times over the years is how important it is for others to hear our story. We both wanted to one day publish and tell others about the trials and successes of fighting for institutional change but given our positions on campus as well as our family responsibilities, we let this desire slip by the wayside. We were also both very aware that initiating these changes had led to a few burned bridges, so we felt the need to tread lightly at times.

During a conversation in 2017 with our colleague, and now co-editor, Amanda McLellan, she reminded us that our story was probably very similar to what others have experienced in libraries and institutions across the country. Amanda M.'s involvement with inclusion and diversity advocacy on campus gave us the extra confidence we needed to pursue this book. It was because of our experience that we sought to develop this anthology with examples of how others are taking steps to improve the library workplace. While there are brainstorming sessions, meetings, data, and more that set the tone for how we will meet our patrons' needs, we tend to push our own needs as employees to the side.

It is not surprising that library staff have a tendency to ignore their personal needs to better serve their patrons. However, this can foster low morale, increase turnover, and create an environment of disenchantment for both employees and patrons. While there is a great deal of existing literature on the importance of advocating and providing for our patrons, it is equally important that we advocate for our own needs as well as those of our colleagues. This anthology was created to gain insights from individuals in various positions within libraries. It provides a broad range of experiences and practical information on creating and fostering an inclusive and positive workplace.

This empowering collection should be useful to current and future library employees and could be applicable to other service-oriented workplaces. It is an anthology that supports and encourages the sharing of knowledge and experiences and encourages action when there is an opportunity for change. The chapters included here are written by library employees from their own unique perspectives and experiences, and, in turn, both administrators and frontline staff obtain ideas and devise actionable steps to implement positive changes, increase morale, and create an engaging and inclusive workspace. The chapters in this anthology address challenges faced by employees in community college, law, special, and university library settings, as well as the steps and outcomes needed for overcoming those challenges. It includes a diverse range of case studies, narratives, and personal essays that identify challenges and offer potential solutions. Overall, it is a collection of ideas and of solutions, many of which could be applicable to any institution that serves the community.

We all need to accept that it is essential for employees to advocate for the needs of those who work in libraries as strongly as we do for our patrons. When we are able to accomplish this, we are not only creating a better workplace, but a better future for everyone. Ironically, Amanda V. and I have not directly benefited from the many changes in lactation accommodations on campus; however, we have had the opportunity to see the positive changes firsthand. I have a daughter who graduated from East Carolina University in May 2019. She spent many hours of the last four years at Joyner Library working on her degree. She also became a mother herself. She was able to continue her studies uninterrupted due in part to the available lactation room at Joyner. Research, analysis, and sheer tenacity can sometimes make the difference between the growth of a thriving library community and merely occupying space within a building. In the end, change takes time and requires fierce tenacity, but it is certainly worth it.

ACKNOWLEDGMENTS

Amanda McLellan would like to thank her husband, Jason, for always supporting her no matter what madness she cooks up. She would also like to thank all of the authors who contributed their stories, and her co-editors whose hard work really inspired the creation of this book to begin with.

Amanda Vinogradov would like to thank her husband, Sergey, and her daughter, Zoe, for their support. From making sure she had the time to hide out in the study room for late night edits, to helpfully taking notes on Mama's laptop, you have been her greatest strength. She would also like to thank the authors who contributed their stories, and who were so wonderful to work with. And finally, words cannot express how thankful she is for her incredibly talented co-editors.

Heather Seibert would like to thank her husband, Tim; her children, Ashlyn, Tara, Helena, Silas, and her granddaughter "Lily Bell" for their love and support. They are a daily reminder as to why it is so important to fight for what is right. Additionally, she would like to sincerely thank Marcia S., Jody K., Melissa H., Ginger B. and Judy Spain for being examples of strong women and teaching her the importance of finding her "people." She would also like to extend a special thank you to her baby brother Brian for always being the hero she needs when things get tough; "Most." And finally, she would like to thank the co-editors of this book, and she is very honored to be a part of the "bi-tri-winning" team.

The editors would like to extend their sincerest thanks to those who supported this publication and all that it entailed. We would like to thank Patrick, our editor, and ALA Publishing for believing in this anthology enough to give it a chance. Thank you, Patrick, for your patience and encouragement while helping us navigate publishing, and for answering our many questions. We would also like to extend our thanks and respect to the contributing authors of this anthology. We are inspired by your actions and your motivation to create and implement change. We would like to extend a special thank-you to everyone that supported Heather and Amanda V. in advocating for lactation accommodations at ECU over the past six years. And finally, we would like to thank Floyd Conner. He is the unsung hero who supported Amanda and Heather in the creation of the Lactation Room at Joyner Library. Your strength and unfaltering pursuit of what is right makes you a driving inspiration for anyone who seeks to improve their workplace and lives; we appreciate and see you.

Do You Want Change with That?

Identifying Lactation Needs and Solutions in Academic Libraries

Heather Seibert, *National Heritage Academy*
Amanda Vinogradov, *special collections cataloging, East Carolina University*

What Existed (2012)

I n 2012, while working in Technical Services at Joyner Library, East Carolina University (ECU), Amanda Vinogradov and I discovered that we would
both be expecting a child in the spring of 2013. In the fall of that year, we
approached our administration to inform them that we would need lactation
accommodations after returning from maternity leave. We discovered that
there were only two lactation rooms available on East Carolina University's
campus. The room nearest to us was still too far away from our workstations
to be feasible, so we were assigned a study room on the third floor of Joyner
Library. Notably, this was one officially designated lactation room for approximately 15,000 people at East Carolina University in 2013 (OED, 2018).

We were only allowed to keep the room locked during the workday, but
outside of those hours we were sharing this space with the public. Thus, we
encountered issues with sanitation, privacy, room scheduling, and access.
These issues included, but were not limited to, constant interruptions from
patrons during pumping times, as well as mucus, rotten food, and other
unmentionable bodily fluids left on the desk and walls of the room we were
using for pumping. These deterrents, combined with the constant need for
the space to be "reset for use," continuously interrupted the short amount
of time that we were allowed to pump. Our building operations staff were
wonderful throughout all of this and did their best to help us through this

difficult time. Unfortunately, as a result of these barriers, I stopped pumping for my son after 10 months—short of the time frame protected by the law. There was little help from the university in terms of resources or information, so we began looking into what rights we might have under the 2010 Patient Protection and Affordable Care Act.

We discovered that the Affordable Care Act (ACA) had amended sections of the Fair Labor Standards Act (FLSA) to require "a place, other than a bathroom, that is shielded from view and free from intrusion from coworkers and the public, which may be used by an employee to express breast milk" (USDL, 2018). We then reviewed legal interpretations to get a sense of how North Carolina employers were adapting their workplace policies and spaces to accommodate the ACA and the changes it had made to the FLSA (Rangel, 2010). Research has continuously proven that the changes made by the ACA has increased overall breastfeeding rates across the country, likely due to the protections it has created for lactating employees.

We also began making comparisons between ECU and institutions across the state, including other UNC system schools. We did this first out of curiosity, but it quickly became clear that ECU had fallen behind many of the schools in the state in terms of lactation accommodations, support, and compliance.

Our Response (2014)

We first proposed the creation of a lactation room within Joyner Library at a Staff Assembly meeting in early 2014. A key point in our proposal was that the room would be used for lactation accommodations exclusively, so that future users of the room could avoid some of the difficulties we had encountered. Unfortunately, we met with some resistance to this idea. Not being the type of people to give up easily, we immediately began investigating ways to break down the barriers that ECU had created for working mothers.

We started gathering supporting evidence that workplace lactation support reduced absenteeism, reduced use of sick leave, and improved employee retention and morale. Incredibly, we discovered that there was an abundance of research available demonstrating the benefits of these programs for businesses. The small cost of devoting a space and resources to lactation accommodations was more than made up for with improvements in these various measures.

As library staff, we knew that ECU wanted to position itself as an institution that was supportive and accepting of non-traditional students, adult learners, and student veterans. There are even specific goals in place to improve outreach services to these populations. The university also wishes to be "recognized as a family friendly workplace" (ECU, 2017). Nevertheless, this desired image was completely at odds with our experiences and with the general lack of resources on campus for nursing mothers.

Advocating for the creation of a lactation room at Joyner, as well as an additional room on campus, seemed like a tremendous opportunity to not only satisfy a basic need for university employees, but also a chance to go a step further and look at best practices in this area. The university could strive to be the best in these accommodations over and above its peer institutions. This was already a niche that ECU was trying to occupy and it is always easier to sell broad institutional changes when there is a demonstrated opportunity for advancement. As staff, we could work to fulfill the university's mission through the development of a comprehensive lactation support program on campus, rather than attempt to meet the minimum standards of support established by law.

In our first step towards working with the greater campus community (rather than confining the issue to our own space), we began an email conversation on March 21, 2014, with our staff senate representative, our assistant director, and our human resources (HR) representative in the library. We provided them with all our research, various best practice guidelines related to workplace support, room design, and peer institution comparisons. Our Staff Senate representative then communicated our concerns about lactation accommodations on campus to the ECU Staff Senate. We should note here that Amanda and I both had quit trying to pump for our children and provide milk for them during the day before we proposed the creation of the lactation room in Joyner Library in 2014. At this point, it was pure stubbornness and a desire to enact the change we wanted to see that kept us moving forward on campus.

In August of 2014, a West Campus representative requested to meet with us. She was working to secure space for a lactation room on the Health Sciences Campus, which required her to provide the university's Space Planning Committee with justification for the use of space, as well as guidelines for the space design. We provided her with copies of the materials that we had gathered, including information regarding the relevant laws on expressing breastmilk at work, best practice guidelines for workplace lactation support programs, policies, and sample space accommodations of our peer institutions. A lactation room was added on West Campus later that year. However, it is important to note that the campus as a whole was not investigating best practice guidelines for room design or overall lactation support.

At this time, Amanda and I were classified as "non-faculty" employees subject to the N.C. State Human Resources Act and did not have voting rights or the representation to suggest large-scale change. We would most likely have never been able to effect change on the scale we did without the support of our colleagues and administration at Joyner Library. In late 2014, our library director enabled SHRA employees (non-faculty) at the library to play a greater role in institutional decision-making by enacting Staff Shared Governance at Joyner Library. After this change, SHRA staff in the library were included in meetings and allowed to serve on more decision-making committees. The director opened new lines of communication that provided staff with an avenue to express their concerns and have a say in the way decisions and projects were implemented at the library. Due to these changes, we were able to move forward with our work without being limited by our employee classification.

We realized how crucial it was to tie in our advocacy efforts to a broad, campus-wide movement, rather than limiting our focus to the needs of library employees. I was elected to Staff Senate as the academic affairs staff representative, and also became HR chair elect. This was a pivotal moment that allowed us to turn the conversations on campus away from temporary accommodations and towards establishing best practice guidelines for institutional policies, room design, and support programs. By 2015, a permanent lactation room had been created at Joyner Library. In 2016, we continued our on-campus advocacy efforts as I was elected staff chair of the Chancellor's Committee on the Status of Women (CCSW) while also serving on the Parenting and Pregnancy Committee. While serving as chair of CCSW, I was able to create an official Lactation Committee, currently housed in the Office of Equity and Diversity, to oversee lactation accommodations on campus. I was also able to take part in the development and creation of an official ECU lactation policy while serving on the Parenting and Pregnancy Committee.

While we were advocating as much as possible within the scope of our ability and position, other committees and groups on campus were recognizing the need for creating a change for new mothers on campus. These organizations included, but were not limited to, the Faculty Senate, Faculty Affairs, Women and Gender Studies, Office of Equity and Diversity, and Student Health.

Barriers

To understand why we were able to make so many changes in such a short period of time, it is important to understand and examine the barriers to lactation support we encountered on campus.

1. Space, or the lack thereof, is one of the biggest barriers we faced on campus. There is always a way to come up with a reason not to devote space to a lactation room. We understand the difficulties of space planning on a university campus. Every department has projects or materials requiring space for storage or services. However, the university's employees have to physically exist in these buildings. When lactation accommodations don't exist, physically being on campus becomes very difficult for lactating employees. Notably, this is not just a concern for employees, but also for students, visiting researchers, and conference attendees. Without these accommodations, libraries are essentially excluding people from their physical space.

2. There is still a lot of stigma surrounding breasts (Rose, 2012). Even the word itself can make people uncomfortable. There is a very real stigma against breastfeeding mothers that we see documented on social media, on the news, as well as on campus (Rosen-Carolle, 2018). Over the past few years, we have talked to many lactating mothers or past mothers on campus, and all have a story to tell. Five main points have stood out each time: 1) we were not taken seriously; 2) we feel unsupported; 3) lactation seems like a dirty or taboo subject; 4) much of the criticism of breastfeeding has actually come from women; and 5) women of color on campus reported experiencing more and far harsher criticism after requesting lactation accommodations (Asiodu, 2017).

3. Employee classification can have a measurable effect on an employee's access to adequate lactation accommodations on a university campus. This can be somewhat dependent on the employee's particular department, but it is important to be aware that some classifications or categories of jobs on campus might indicate that person is more likely to be working in a cubicle rather than in an office with a door. Or, they may be working a service desk and be unable to "work through" a lactation break, requiring them to clock out for the entirety of the process. Such differences are important in terms of how people use space in campus buildings and how they have to keep track of their time.

4. It is important to understand the amount of time required for pumping in order to fully comprehend the relationship this has to an employee's ability to continue pumping at work. At a minimum, a pumping session requires 15 minutes of active pumping to adequately empty the breast. Emptying the breast is important not only to provide storable breastmilk for feeding a child, but also to maintain supply and prevent dangerous infections (Spencer, 2008). The amount of milk someone produces is directly related to the length and number of sessions that person is able to breastfeed or pump. In short, the supply will adjust to the demand. Breastfeeding or pumping less than the recommended amount can also cause mastitis, which can require hospitalization. For the lactating employee, student, or campus visitor, breastfeeding or pumping frequently during the day is not optional; it is physically required.

5. Room location can make a huge difference in an employee's ability to pump at work. A ten-minute walk to a lactation room for a tenured faculty member is a completely different experience from an SHRA employee who has to clock out for the entire process. If a pumping session, including walking to and from the room as well as clean-up and milk storage, is at a minimum 25 minutes, adding ten or more minutes of walking to a lactation room creates a significant barrier for any employee that needs to clock out. A lunch break may be used to cover one session; however, this leaves one or more sessions during the day that the employee has to account for somewhere else. Most employees will have exhausted their remaining leave time during maternity leave, so using accrued leave is usually not an option. Some employees may be able to use a flexible schedule, but this is frequently not possible for many reasons. Eventually, some people may get their pay reduced because they can't work the hours to make up the time. Given how expensive childbirth already is in the United States, this can become an insurmountable barrier for many.

6. Another barrier we unfortunately encountered was hostility against our advocacy efforts. Some of this hostility is related to the stigma surrounding breastfeeding, but there is also the perception that people requesting accommodations are attempting to secure special treatment and services. Luckily, most of the time the resistance we encountered was due to a lack of education and training. This was truer a few

years ago on the ECU campus, but it does still apply. When we first began looking into lactation support on campus, most people were not aware of the amended section 7 of the FLSA or what it entailed. Due to increasing room visibility through universal signage, inclusion on the campus map, an updated HR policy, and the occasional mention in our on-campus news service, we do feel that overall campus awareness is improving and believe it will continue to do so.

7. Committees are one of the blessings and curses of working at an academic institution. We have everyone working towards the same goal, but sometimes it takes us awhile to realize that there are others out there working on the same thing from a different angle.

8. Many people have good intentions and want to help, but they have preconceived ideas of what that help should entail. For example, donations like pumps and towels, or assistance in developing private spaces are always appreciated, but tampon dispensers are not going to be needed in a lactation room. Another example of these good intentions would be those who are making a good faith effort to help by trying to meet the minimum standards established by law. This can be a barrier in and of itself. We definitely encountered this in our own experiences at the library, where everyone involved was trying their hardest to make the study room work and it just didn't. It wasn't the right accommodation to our need.

What Exists Now (2018)

When we initially requested accommodations, there were only two spaces devoted to lactation accommodations for the entire campus. Since those humble beginnings in 2012, the Lactation Committee has been able to create nine lactation rooms on campus with others in the planning stage. They have performed room audits, conducted user surveys, created universal signage, and secured updated room furnishings for all rooms. Each room has a minifridge (some were donated while others were purchased). For example, the Friends of Joyner Library purchased the mini fridge in the library's lactation room. Donations of materials for breastfeeding mothers were obtained through various corporate sponsors and these materials are provided free of charge within the lactation rooms across campus. The Lactation Committee has also procured hospital grade pumps for lactating mothers to borrow. These rooms have also been added to the ECU campus maps, dramatically increasing visibility and access for the rooms. Along with the changes, breastfeeding friendly awards have been presented to Joyner Library, Student Health, as well as ECU Family Medicine.

While great strides have been made to dismantle the various barriers to lactating mothers at ECU, there is still need for improvement. With an increasing awareness of the needs of mothers returning to work, various policies have been implemented to make that transition easier. However, there is not a one-size-fits-all approach to meet the needs of those that would need these accommodations. The development and creation of the lactation rooms, the Lactation Committee efforts, and the lactation accommodation policy created by the human resources department have all greatly improved the situation that Amanda and I faced in 2012. Yet, it is imperative that these policies and efforts are continually revisited and developed so that they continue to meet the needs of those that occupy the workplace of the institution.

References

Asiodu, Ifeyinwa V., Catherine M. Waters, Dawn E. Dailey, and Audrey Lyndon. (April 2017). Infant feeding decision-making and the influences of social support persons among first-time African American mothers. *Maternal and Child Health Journal*, *21*(4), 863–72. https://doi.org/10.1007/s10995-016 -2167-x

East Carolina University. (December 4, 2017). ECU Diversity: Workforce Representation. Lactation Support | Version 2 (Current Version) | Policies, Rules and Regulations. Retrieved April 29, 2018 from http://www.ecu.edu/ prr/06/10/02

Kapinos, Kandice A., Lindsey Bullinger, and Tami Gurley-Calvez. (2017). Lactation support services and breastfeeding initiation: Evidence from the Affordable Care Act. *Health Services Research*, *52*(6), 2175–96. https://doi .org/10.1111/1475-6773.12598

Rangel, Charles. (March 23, 2010). H.R.3590 - 111th Congress (2009–2010): Patient Protection and Affordable Care Act. Retrieved from https://www .congress.gov/bill/111th-congress/house-bill/3590

Rose, Lindsey M. (2012). Legally public but privately practiced: Segregating the lactating body. *Health Communication* 27, no. 1. 49–57. https://doi.org/10.108 0/10410236.2011.568999

Rosen-Carole, Casey, Katherine Allen, Maria Fagnano, Ann Dozier, and Jill Halterman. (April 2018). Mothers' concerns for personal safety and privacy while breastfeeding: An unexplored phenomenon. *Breastfeeding Medicine: The Official Journal of the Academy of Breastfeeding Medicine, 13*(3), 181–88. https://doi.org/10.1089/bfm.2017.0187

Spencer, Jeanne P. (September 15, 2008). Management of mastitis in breast-feeding women. *American Family Physician, 78*(6), 727–31.

The Office for Equity and Diversity. (2018). ECU diversity: Historical ECU fall enrollment. Retrieved from https://public.tableau.com/profile/the.office.for.equity.and.diversity#!/vizhome/DRAFTECUDiversity-HistoricalECUFallEnrollment/CoverPage

U.S. Department of Labor. (n.d). Wage and Hour Division (WHD) - Section 7(r) of the Fair Labor Standards Act – Break Time for Nursing Mothers Provision. Retrieved from https://www.dol.gov/whd/nursingmothers/Sec7rFLSA_btnm.htm

Options for New Parents Returning to Work

Tashia Munson, *access services and outreach librarian, University of Michigan*

A t some point, every new parent asks themselves "Can I do this?" as they find themselves on the cusp of returning to work. With whatever medical leave they are provided, new parents learn to redefine what their family is as well as the needs and expectations of their new roles as parents. By the time they return to work, they are fundamentally different people, with new expectations and responsibilities outside of their roles as employees. By no means are these changes limited to first-time parents, as each new child in a family redefines the meaning of what that family is and needs.

Juggling the Baby

In 2017, I gave birth to my youngest daughter. For my entire pregnancy, I planned and prepared for my leave and eventual return to work. What I didn't realize until I returned was that I only made preparations for the first two weeks, that the enormous change in my personal life would have minimal effect on my 9–5 life, or that the addition of a second child to my family would be pretty much the same as being a mom of one. I honestly don't think I have ever been so wrong about something in my entire life.

While I was busy planning and plotting out childcare arrangements, scheduling routine checkups with the doctor, and negotiating my first week back on the job, I neglected to remember that life will inevitably remind you how unpredictable it will be. For me, this took the shape of discovering I was pregnant again only six short sweet months after the birth of my daughter, and in 2018 I welcomed my third child. With my son's birth I was determined to do things differently—for myself, my career, and my family—than I had with my daughter the previous year.

Before Returning to Work

Before I returned to work, I had time to reflect on what worked, and more importantly what didn't work, during my return the previous year. One of the first changes I had to make was in my own expectations. While before I may have thought that I could slide back into my role with little to no interruption, this time around I knew better and I focused on two inarguable facts:

1. I am a fundamentally different person as a mother of three than I had been when I was a mother of two, and that is okay.
2. Although I may have fundamentally changed, my workplace would be frustratingly the same on my return, and that too is okay.

This change in perspective gave me permission to be okay with not fitting in right away, and to take my time to find the new balance I needed for my work life and my family. For me, this meant taking additional time off after my leave ended. For an additional week I was able to take my time to communicate with my partner, family, and friends about what returning to work would look like. This also gave me the opportunity to hear that they needed from me. This open communication and honest discussion about my needs and the needs of those around me continued with my supervisor and colleagues during my first few weeks back at work.

Previously, after my daughter's birth, I would sometimes feel myself getting burned out or overwhelmed by my workload, but I did not have the words to really express what I was experiencing. I was under the presumption that it was just my load to bear and the fact that I could not meant I should just try harder. This stress, coupled with lack of sleep and very questionable eating choices, made me physically ill. Shortly after my return I needed to take several unscheduled sick days.

Knowing that this could happen to me again after my second leave, I decided to be open with my supervisor about my concerns and work out a plan for my return and eventual schedule that took advantage of some of the flexible options available from my organization. The most important options were the abilities to flex my schedule and take personal days for bonding. In my organization, during the first year of employment, a new parent is allowed to take their sick and vacation time for bonding without the need of a doctor's note or other explanation. After an open conversation with my supervisor, I was able to request scheduled half-days every other Tuesday for the year.

A Better Model for Returning Parents

Returning to work after an extended leave, especially a medical leave, is a surreal experience. The first few days will be spent catching up on everything that has changed while you were away, but there also may be an implicit expectation from supervisors or coworkers for you to immediately pick up from where you left off. A better model would be to treat staff returning from extended leave as they would a newly hired employee and provide them with an onboarding period.

There is much debate currently about extending medical leave for parents after the arrival of a new child, but while large public policies may take a long time to become reality, organizations, departments, and supervisors can start to make changes for their own teams now. The first step is to get informed.

Getting Informed

What have other returning parents said they needed from their organizations when they returned? From their supervisors or colleagues? What are supervisors obligated to provide and what will they have to advocate for on behalf of their returning employees to feel supported? Finding answers to these questions can help prepare supervisors wading through unfamiliar territory when their employees return. Reaching out to peers who have been on either side of this situation to talk about their experiences can help supervisors start to think about strategies for their own employees.

Develop a (Realistic) Plan

Be it two weeks or two months, no matter how much time a new parent has been away for their leave it isn't enough. Until such time comes when parents are able to stay with their child *and* keep their jobs, new parents will typically return to work before they ready. Supervisors can help with this transition by communicating and coming up with a transition plan. This plan can include a list of modified duties, flexible hours for the transition period, and discussions on upcoming medical appointments for parents and children.

With the birth of my son coming so soon after my daughter's birth, I knew that having a new baby would mean additional doctor's appointments and require me to be open with my supervisor about my needs. While new parents may not know what their needs are until they need them, the most important thing a supervisor can do in these times is be present and to listen. Supervisors need to take a step beyond "Tell me if there is anything I can do for you," as such platitudes begin to ring hollow if there is no real evidence of support behind the words. Sitting down to work on a plan for their transition, future, and all the life in between demonstrates the kind of support that returning parents can depend on. Advocating on their behalf when the final decision is beyond your control is another. With so much of their new lives out of their control, returning parents need to feel and see support from their workplace.

Doing What's Best for You

Sometimes the place you return to is no longer the place where you need to be. By understanding your own priorities and how your new life will continue to change, you may find yourself in a position to make a difficult decision. No matter what you choose to ensure that your family is in the best possible situation, just remember that it too is okay.

The Campaign for Paid Parental Leave at a Private University

Emily Scharf, *head of reference and instruction,*
Laurence McKinley Gould Library at Carleton College
Heidi Vix, *head of resources management services, Webster University*

Webster University

This case study takes place at Webster University, a comprehensive university whose main campus is in St. Louis, Missouri, USA. Webster has campuses in six other countries, a robust online program, and campuses in metro areas and on military bases in the United States. The majority of Webster students are graduate students and the full-time equivalent (FTE) number is approximately 9,000 students. Webster University Libraries serve students, faculty, and staff around the world, and librarians have opportunities to join committees, task forces, and serve the university in other ways.

Webster Staff Alliance

Webster University Staff Alliance is a counterpart to the Faculty Senate, a body that advocates for the staff at the university. This committee is made up of staff from around the university, and for more than ten years, this group has brought forth proposals to University Administration regarding staff compensation and benefits. In 2017, a librarian serving on the Compensation Committee also had experience serving on the Women, Gender, and Sexuality Studies Committee at the university and because of this was privy to concerns from both faculty and staff around paid parental leave. It was from the two committees and listening to colleagues' own experiences that the librarian and her colleagues on the Compensation Committee wanted to propose paid parental leave for staff to attempt to equalize benefits given to staff to those given to faculty. Later in this case study, the policy differences will be outlined more broadly.

In discussions with the Compensation Committee, it was unclear at first how much leave to request. Policies across higher education institutions varied widely and although parity between faculty and staff was the goal, the committee was unsure if that was possible. After consideration and research within the committee, the Webster Staff Alliance 2017–2018 Compensation Proposal recommended a paid parental leave policy for staff members to minimize the disparity between faculty and staff parental leaves. Faculty could receive as much as 16 weeks or a full semester of paid parental leave, while staff had to rely on vacation and sick time only for payment. Some staff are also not eligible for FMLA, so their leave is solely dependent on the amount of paid time off. In order to better balance the benefits between the two groups of employees, the committee recommended creating a paid staff parental leave policy that included a six-week paid leave to be taken anytime during the six months following a birth, adoption, or foster-care child placement (Webster Staff Alliance, 2017). The University Administration responded that they were open to the idea, pending further research (Schuster & Schmutz, 2017).

Task Force

The WSA Compensation Committee chairperson on the Webster Staff Alliance formed a task force around paid parental leave for staff in June of 2017. The task force was charged with doing research on 10–12 other universities who currently offer paid parental leave for staff members, and then, by early fall 2017, providing its final proposal/recommendation to the Office of Human Resources.

The importance of this work and the short timeline were very good motivators for the team, which was made up of full-time staff. The task force was well represented by various areas of the university, with staff who were not previously affiliated with WSA from the Walker School of Business, School of Education, Global Marketing and Communications, Library, and Athletics Department. Some of these staff members had taken parental leave in the past and had to rely on their paid time off and FMLA.

The task force immediately started working on the charge of reviewing staffing compensation at 20 peer institutions as well as additional local St. Louis institutions. Each university was reviewed using a form to assess current benefits to primary parent, secondary parent, short-term disability, and service requirements. Many of the institutions had information available online. For those that did not, the task force reached out via phone and/or email to their HR department. Most were very accommodating and willing to help Webster University.

Throughout the research process, the chair of the task force was in constant contact with the Webster University human resources director of benefits and compensation. The latter worked with the insurance company to get feedback on how they would coordinate with a parental leave policy. Our insurance company, Prudential, provided a University Paid Parental Leave Benchmarking Analysis. They referenced a 2016 World at Work Survey and a 2016 Society for Human Resource Management (SHRM) survey, which showed the following:

- 13–14 percent of all employers offer a paid parental leave benefit. However, the larger the organization, the more likely it offers a program.
- 54 percent of employers offer less than six weeks of paid leave.
- 37 percent of employers offer between six and 12 weeks of paid leave.
- The survey indicated that leaves for non-birth parents tend to be half as long as leaves for birth mothers.
- Adoptive/Surrogate parents receive approximately 30 days of paid leave.
- 44 percent of employers require 12 months of tenure before use of paid leave.
- 47 percent allow use of paid leave within one year of becoming a parent, with 38 percent requiring use within the first six months.

The task force focused not only on keeping up with other institutions, but also on what all staff should expect after the birth of a child. They found that the recommendations from physicians include a leave of six weeks (American College of Obstetricians and Gynecologists. Executive Board, 2016). They also found that the majority of daycares would not accept children until they are at least six weeks old.

The task force met with the Office of Human Resources several times to better understand the cost impact to the university. After reviewing the parental leave policies of other institutions and the recommendations from physicians, and understanding limitations of the Office of Human Resources and staff members, the task force started brainstorming ideas for the parental leave policy at Webster University. These included asking for eight weeks for the primary caregiver and as little as three weeks for the secondary caregiver with various benefits. The task force also considered how the policy would cover miscarriages, stillbirths, and surrogate mothers.

Within the task force's research, they found that many institutions encourage their staff to use short-term disability to assist with parental leave. Short-term disability covers four weeks leave at 60 percent pay, which would assist Webster University with some of the burden, but only if staff already had short-term disability as part of their insurance package. Getting short-term disability after they have worked at Webster for more than a month was not a guarantee. The task force recommended that the Office of Human Resources strongly encourage all employees to take this option and explain why short-term disability is important.

Draft Policy

In August 2017, the task force started a draft of the paid parental leave policy recommendations that included a summary of the recommendation, a chart of the leave timeline, the rationale (which included faculty's current leave policy, the university's mission, maintaining competitive standing, recommendations by physicians, reasonable cost to the university, and service requirements), and scenarios to show the benefits of taking intermittent leave.

TABLE 3.1
Parental leave benefit

	Weeks 1–4	Weeks 5–8	Weeks 9–12
Primary Parent (includes birth, adoption, surrogates, and stillbirths)	15 day wait	Short-term disability (estimate, wks 3–7)	
	Paid Parental Leave (8 wks, last 2 intermittent)		
	Family Medical and Leave Act (12 wks)		
Secondary Parent (includes miscarriages)	Paid Parental Leave (4 wks intermittent)		
	Family Medical and Leave Act (12 weeks)		

After additional meetings with the Office of Human Resources, the task force realized that not all personnel were interested in moving this policy forward. The task force was prepared with thoughtful, organized, and justified answers to questions from human resources staff. After these meetings, human resources started discussing implementation at the university.

The Office of Human Resources took the recommendations of the task force and made alterations to better fit the financial demands of the university, as well as insurance requirements. Some of the significant differences between the recommendation and the final policy include: the minimum work requirement increased from one year to two years; no mention of miscarriages, stillbirths, or surrogates; the primary parent receives six weeks paid leave instead of eight; and a provision requiring reimbursement if the employee does not return to work within 30 days after the end of the FMLA and paid leave. Some of the policy changes were also expanded benefits; for example, the final policy includes foster child placement as an eligible event for paid parental leave. The policy also gives six weeks of leave to the secondary parent, whereas the task force only recommended four. The policy also included a non-retaliation clause to ensure that all who use the leave would have no reprisal from their department, co-workers, or supervisor.

By November 6, 2017, Webster University had a completed parental leave policy for administrators and staff. The policy was put in place to take effect on January 1, 2018 and remains in place with no changes. The task force plans to ask for a review after a full year to see if the policy could be updated to include the original suggestions from the task force. Normally that is done by including a request for an update in the Webster Staff Alliance Compensation Committee's annual compensation proposal (Webster Staff Alliance, 2019).

References

American College of Obstetricians and Gynecologists. Executive Board. (2016). Paid parental leave. Retrieved from https://www.acog.org/-/media/Statements -of-Policy/Public/92ParentalLeaveJuly2016.pdf?dmc= 1&ts=20170817T1432 02883

Schuster, J. Z., & Schmutz, B. M. (2017). Response to WSA compensation proposal fiscal year 2017-2018. Webster University. Retrieved from http:// www.webster.edu/documents/wsa/compensation-proposals/fy1718-leader ship-response-to-wsa-compensation-proposal.pdf

Society for Human Resource Management. (2016). Paid leave in the workplace. Retrieved from https://www.shrm.org/hr-today/trends-and-forecasting/research-and-surveys/Documents/2016-Paid-Leave-in-the-Workplace.pdf

Webster Staff Alliance. (2017). WSA compensation proposal fiscal year 2017-2018. Retrieved from http://www.webster.edu/documents/wsa/compensation-proposals/fy1718-wsa-compensation-proposal.pdf

Webster Staff Alliance. (2019). Publications. Retrieved from www.webster.edu/wsa/news.html

Chat Reference and Work-Life Balance

Rachel M. Minkin, *head of reference services, Michigan State University*

S ally* (names changed), a single parent of two, balances school closures due to weather and holidays, as well as evening/weekend reference responsibilities. Michael* looked forward to parental leave and needed a way to transition slowly back into full-time work while also continuing to assist his partner in childcare and taking their newborn to appointments. And then there are some of us who are in the "sandwich" generation, caring for our younger children as well as our aging parents, spending time in parents' homes and doctors' offices yet needing to preserve vacation time for our children's inevitable school closures and illnesses.

Work-Life Balance refers to employees finding compatibility between their work lives and their personal lives with the expectation that both the employee and the corporation will benefit from this balance, a boon for hiring and retention. Work-Life Balance (sometimes called Work-Life Flexibility) encompasses disciplines ranging from Business and Labor Relations to Psychology and Sociology to Religion and Health, but all focus on what it means for employees to balance these two aspects of their lives. Michigan State University's (MSU) WorkLife Office speaks of "honoring your work and personal lives," while recognizing that honoring both may not mean a 50-50 split between the two lives. With this in mind, I write this chapter as head of reference services at MSU Libraries (MSUL), as well as a parent, daughter, and spouse. I feel that chat reference allows MSUL to honor our work and personal lives in the spirit of the MSU WorkLife Office.

The Telecommuting Librarian

Chat reference provides library reference staff with an option to cover service points even while they are out of the building. As salaried faculty, MSU librarians are not asked to be in the building at set times, with the exception of those librarians covering service points (i.e., reference services). Although a typical reference assignment is only approximately ten hours a week, this required service can prove difficult for working parents or those caring for elderly or ill family members (as it would be for any teaching faculty). Balancing desk reference with chat reference allows flexing schedules to accommodate those needs. Chat reference, then, is a form of telecommuting. If we choose to look at chat reference in this manner, we can then visualize it as a means to a more compassionate work-life balance—providing the flexibility to work *and* be present for loved ones and appointments, balancing the needs of staff with the needs of the library.

Platforms and Services

Chat reference (also called virtual reference) benefits library patrons by providing information at point of need *and* while patrons are already online searching. Much has been written on the analysis of the chat transcript, the value of the service to online student success, and gleaning data through mining transcripts (see many recent articles, including Brown, 2017, Peters, 2018 and Prieto, 2017). In Michigan, chat reference also benefits academic libraries as a whole, as evidenced by the long-standing chat collaborative, Research Help Now (RHN), comprised of 15 member institutions. I feel we should also highlight benefits to reference staff; that is, explicitly pointing out the freedom to staff and engage from any space with suitable internet connections, including one's home.

MSUL participates in a collaborative chat service, Research Help Now (RHN). Utilizing OCLC's QuestionPoint (QP) software, MSUL staff, along with 14 other Michigan academic institutions, set hours in which we monitor each other's chat services, as well as the 24/7 QP chat services. Together for approximately 15 years, the collaboration benefits patrons by providing increased chat staffing levels—by pooling all our staffing, RHN provides (nearly) local chat reference 85–90 hours a week. With the largest student FTE (and the biggest staff) of the collaborative, MSUL covers a large portion of collaborative chat hours. MSUL reference services benefits from our expanded chat hours, as chat reference seems to be a favorite mode for MSUL patrons. At MSU, chat reference is used much more often than in-person (desk) reference, demonstrating 256 percent growth in questions asked from fall 2016 to fall 2017. Our patrons benefit from public services that are more expertise based, more decentralized, and incredibly valuable as they extend expertise beyond the 9–5 physical location.

Within the RHN collaborative, other member institutions are also demonstrating chat usage increases. For smaller institutions, chat has been a benefit not only to their patrons, but also as a way to market and advocate for their libraries within their larger organizations. These smaller libraries point to their increasing patron statistics (regardless of who answered the individual questions) as a reminder of their value within the academic system.

Serving Patrons *and* Staff

With most of the emphasis on the value of chat reference to patrons and libraries, we overlook the value to library reference staff. As with telecommuting in the corporate sector, chat reference often takes place outside of the traditional point of physical reference, the desk. In fact, at MSUL, we discourage reference staff from providing chat reference concurrently with desk service. Needing only a good internet connection and adequate Wi-Fi, chat reference happens at cafes, homes, offices, and even outdoors.

In order to promote a good work-life fit, we can tout this fact rather than bury it. At MSUL, all reference librarians are quarter time assigned, and yet they are there by their own volition. Reference staff are quarter time in MSUL reference services because they want to be, enjoying not only their work with our patrons but also the flexibility afforded them. We can also promote this flexibility to future library staff, perhaps offering flexible chat reference experience to LIS graduate students from our two in-state LIS programs and the plethora of in-state students pursuing online degrees through other LIS programs.

Objections

There is some backlash to chat reference as a means to work-life balance. Anecdotally, some MSUL supervisors feel it is unfair to allow any work from home and that librarians should be physically at work, either in our building or working in their liaison areas' buildings. These supervisors are concerned that if a librarian is at home, then they are not truly working, spending more time on personal things. Although one could certainly abuse this system, chat reference is active telecommuting. Because of the increase in patrons choosing chat reference, reference staff are not sitting and staring at a blank screen waiting. Rather, we see a steady stream of transcripts and data, evidence for supervisors who need to see the legitimacy of this work. (As mentioned above, this is one of the reasons why we do not allow reference desk staff to simultaneously cover chat reference—it's too busy!)

Conversely, for those legally at home (for example, those on parental leave), an option to work at home may encourage a tendency to do work even when a reference staff should not be. We cannot legally allow reference staff on leave to continue working. However, we can allow reference staff to decide how they would like to allocate their leave, allowing them the flexibility to extend their leave by working from home in small increments; that is, a two-hour chat shift. They can then add two hours on at the tail end of their leave. Additionally, as with caring for aging parents, reference staff may not need a full leave but rather the flexibility of not being tied to a desk for set periods of time.

Chat reference is an important part of reference services for many libraries, benefitting patrons and libraries as a whole. Chat reference is also an important part of reference staff work-life balance, allowing flexibility in lieu of a traditionally desk-based service. Our patrons also benefit by allowing them access to expertise without having to leave their research space. Our libraries benefit too, by allowing their institutions to hire and retain talented library staff. Most importantly, reference staff benefits through an honoring of their work and personal lives.

References

Brown, R. (2017). Lifting the veil: Analyzing collaborative virtual reference transcripts to demonstrate value and make recommendations for practice. *Reference & User Services Quarterly*, 57(1), 42–47. https://doi.org/10.5860/rusq.57.1.6441

Michigan State University. (n.d.). MSU WorkLife Office. Retrieved from https://worklife.msu.edu/

Peters, T. (2018). Online students use of virtual reference services. *Journal of Electronic Resources Librarianship*, 30(1), 1–8. https://doi.org/10.1080/1941126X.2018.1443901

Prieto, A. G. (2017). Humanistic perspectives in virtual reference. *Library Review*, *66*(8/9), 695–710. https://doi.org/10.1108/LR-01-2017-0005

Further Reading

Armann-Keown, V., Cooke, C. A., and Matheson, G. (2015). Digging deeper into virtual reference transcripts. *Reference Services Review*, 43(4), 656–672. https://doi.org/10.1108/RSR-04-2015-0024

Coughenour, A. D. (2017). Virtual Reference in a Global Context: Going Beyond Local Needs. *Internet Reference Services Quarterly*, *22*(1), 55–62. https://doi.org/10.1080/10875301.2016.1276992

McKewan, J., & Richmond, S. S. (2017). Needs and results in virtual reference transactions: A longitudinal study. *The Reference Librarian*, *58*(3), 179–189. https://doi.org/10.1080/02763877.2016.1233086

Nydegger, R. (2018). *Clocking in: The psychology of work*. Santa Barbara, California: Greenwood.

United States Office of Personnel Management. (2018). The federal work-life survey government wide report (No. ES/SESPM-03025-03/2018) (88 pages). Washington, DC. Retrieved from https://permanent.access.gpo.gov/gpo89913/2018-federal-work-life-survey-report.pdf

5

Making Room for Working Mothers
Lactation and Breastfeeding at Emory University

Meaghan O'Riordan, *accessioning and collections manager, Emory University*
Dorothy Waugh, *digital archivist, Emory University*

In 2015, Emory's university librarian established a Wellness Committee, charged with developing and supporting programs and resources promoting wellness among staff in Emory's Library and IT Services (LITS) division. Since its inception, the committee has organized mindfulness workshops, launched a "LITS Colors" program in which coloring stations are made available to staff as a means of stress relief, promoted walking groups and 5K charity runs, and championed university-wide efforts related to health and wellness. In 2018, members of the Wellness Committee were contacted by staff concerned about the lack of a dedicated lactation space in the library, which, on average, welcomes just under 9,000 people every day, including Emory students, faculty, and visitors, and is staffed by over 220 Emory employees.

An Inadequate Family Lounge

For several years, staff at the Robert W. Woodruff Library had voiced concerns over the lack of a suitable space for breastfeeding and lactation inside the library building. The existing space was situated within a wide corridor leading to a women's bathroom on the building's third floor. Folding screens were used to delineate the space, which contained an armchair and small table. A sign outside identified the space as a "Family Lounge," although it was regularly used by visitors to the library as a quiet space for reading, relaxing, or conducting phone calls. Women in need of a place to pump breastmilk expressed frustration at the lack of privacy afforded by the space and the lack of clarity regarding its purpose. In 2015, these issues were brought to the attention of the Library Employee Advocacy Forum (LEAF), a committee formed in the 1970s to represent library employees and serve as their liaison to library leadership. In response, members of LEAF reviewed Emory's policy governing lactation support for breastfeeding faculty (http://policies.emory .edu/4.91), staff and students, and, over the course of the next two years, worked closely with the Center for Women at Emory to audit the existing space and propose some options for improved lactation support at the library.

The audit of the existing family lounge identified four areas where the space failed to comply with Emory's policy:

- There wasn't any signage indicating that the space was intended for breastfeeding or lactation.
- Contact details as to where users of the space could direct questions or concerns were not posted.
- The space had no outlets, which are essential for many electric breast pumps.
- Finally, as a result of the space's configuration, it had no door, no lock, and consequently failed to provide adequate levels of privacy.

In addition to these compliance issues, the report recommended that hand sanitizer, paper towels, and, if possible, a hospital-grade breast pump be provided.

The pressing need for a lockable door and floor-to-ceiling privacy required that either the existing space be renovated or an alternative space found. Members of LEAF proposed repurposing another room in the building as a dedicated lactation space, but this was met with some resistance. As is often the case on university campuses, physical space within the library is in high demand, and competing priorities for rooms in the building hindered efforts to locate a new space. LEAF explored the possibility of purchasing a freestanding, mobile lactation pod, but costs were prohibitive. As a result, while LEAF was able to make improvements to the existing space in terms of signage, efforts to provide a dedicated, private space understandably stalled.

When the LITS Wellness Committee was contacted about this issue in late 2018, we joined forces with LEAF and set out to establish whether changes within the library over the previous 18 months might help us regain some traction. Armed with notes and research generously provided by LEAF, the

Wellness Committee approached Emory's university librarian again to share the feedback that we too had now heard. The response was largely positive. In 2015, Emory Libraries had entered a phase of master planning, aimed at evaluating the ways in which library spaces are organized and used. This work was reaching fruition around the time of our meeting with the university librarian, and library administration was keen to incorporate a new lactation room into plans based on the audit's findings. A timeline for this project, however, was not yet confirmed and completion of this work was likely several years away. In the meantime, a temporary solution was necessary. Given the probability that large-scale renovations throughout the library building might soon occur as the result of master planning, library administration was understandably reluctant to invest in short-term renovations of the existing lactation space. One alternative possibility was that an existing graduate student study be repurposed as a lactation room, but these studies are in high demand throughout the school year and there were concerns among some library staff about losing a graduate study in order to provide a lactation space. In order to address some of these concerns, the LITS Wellness Committee planned a focus group in which interested parties could contribute to this ongoing conversation.

Focus Group

In February 2018, we invited Emory's university librarian and a representative from Emory's Center for Women to participate in our focus group aimed at gathering feedback on the existing lactation space and proposals for creating a new space. All LITS staff were invited to participate. A representative from LEAF attended to provide context based on their previous work, and a colleague from the Emory Center for Women provided clarification on Emory's policy and assisted in making recommendations for changes to the space. Our intention was to provide our university librarian with the opportunity to hear directly from staff and ask questions that would allow her to make an informed decision about if and how resources could be allocated to create a new, dedicated lactation room. While open to all staff, many in attendance were using or had previously used the existing lactation space at the library. These participants provided valuable insight as to some of the problems associated with the current space. We, as organizers, were also cognizant that the proposed lactation space should serve students and visitors to the library, in addition to staff alone, and tried to ensure that the discussion took these additional users into consideration.

The primary concern voiced by participants was the lack of privacy afforded by the existing space. Because there was no lock, staff often had to ask students and visitors using the space for other purposes to leave. This caused discomfort and made staff feel awkward. Furthermore, staff who had previously used the space reported that the lack of a lock left them feeling exposed. Participants emphasized the importance of a convenient and suitably equipped location at which to pump in order to cause the least amount of disruption to their workday. They noted that pumping takes time even given the best of circumstances, but that the existing space's lack of appropriate facilities to support women during pumping and for appropriate storage for pump pieces and milk added significantly to this time. In addition to the anxiety caused by the space's lack of privacy, the space was considered inconvenient and difficult to use.

Having voiced their concerns, members of the focus group were invited to provide recommendations for improvements to the space. It was our hope that these recommendations would inform both the eventual creation of dedicated, purpose-built lactation room(s) during renovations of the library building and a temporary room, repurposed to conform with Emory's lactation support policy until renovations are completed. Many of the proposed recommendations echoed the findings of the Center for Women's audit of the existing space and the requirements established by Emory's policy. In particular, participants re-emphasized the importance of a lock. In order to make the space accessible to everyone, including students and visitors, the group recommended that access to the room be controlled using a coded lockbox and that the code be made accessible at all the service desks in the library. Participants requested a comfortable armchair, a table upon which to set up pumps and associated pieces, access to electrical outlets, a lamp to avoid harsh overhead lighting, a refrigerator, and a sink, preferably located inside the room. Having recognized the challenges involved in incorporating time for pumping into a busy working day, the group also requested a reliable Wi-Fi signal in order to facilitate multitasking.

In addition to these recommendations, the group made suggestions that we agreed might be difficult to accommodate in a temporary space, but which we hope will be integrated into plans for permanent lactation rooms during library renovations. Participants requested that the new space be designed to accommodate multiple users at one time. One option that received a very positive response imagined a dedicated and fully enclosed central space with sinks, lockers, and a refrigerator, from which users have access to individual, lockable rooms, furnished according to Emory policy. The group also suggested that some kind of booking system be made available in order to help women plan their day and make the most efficient use of their time. Having discussed the possibility that this space be used for breastfeeding, in addition to pumping, participants recommended that a changing table and the appropriate trash cans be provided. Finally, the group reflected on how important it is that women feel comfortable and relaxed while using any lactation space and recommended that this be a key consideration in any future design plans.

Creating the Space

Overall, the focus group meeting proved to be extremely productive. The call for a new lactation space met with a very positive response from all attendees. At the conclusion of the meeting, our university librarian committed to providing a temporary space by the summer of 2018, if not before, and re-emphasized that a permanent and dedicated lactation space will be an intentional part of the library renovations planned over the next several years.

Following the focus group meeting, our university librarian met her commitment to a temporary space very quickly. A room was identified by mid-March, and, in consultation with the Wellness Committee chair, it was quickly outfitted according to many of the recommendations outlined by focus group participants. Additional stakeholders were invited to view the room and offer feedback and the temporary space was made available to everyone in May 2018.

The temporary space is a repurposed graduate student study situated in a public stacks area with floor-to-ceiling walls and a door that locks. The key is stored in a lockbox outside of the room alongside a sign that clearly identifies the room as a lactation space. Staff, students, and visitors to the library can request the access code at any of the library service desks. Inside the room is a large, comfortable armchair, a floor lamp, and a small table. Paper towels and cleaning wipes are provided and the trash can is emptied regularly. There are several outlets in the space, as well as reliable Wi-Fi access. There is a refrigerator for convenient storage of milk and pump parts and the room is located close to an ADA-compliant restroom with a sink. Contact information for the room's manager is posted inside the room, as well as a copy of the university's lactation support policy, and brochures providing additional information about support and resources for working mothers at Emory are available there, too.

Since its opening, the new temporary space has been incredibly well received. Staff have observed that the provision of a lockable room alone has resulted in a space that feels safer, while the additional features, such as the refrigerator, armchair, and electrical outlets, have provided comfort and important functionality. In September 2018, the Emory Center for Women assessed the temporary space and reported that it now conforms to Emory's lactation support policy. Their documentation and promotional resources have been updated accordingly.

Our long-term goal remains that further improvements be incorporated into the design and implementation of a permanent, dedicated lactation space as part of the library's upcoming renovations. The library has made great progress with the creation of the temporary space, but with additional improvements, such as more immediate access to a sink for cleaning pump parts and the ability to accommodate more than one user at a time, the library's lactation space could lead the way for other departments and buildings on campus. We are grateful to our university librarian for her responsiveness to staff concerns and her commitment to supporting working mothers at Emory. The temporary space is an incredible improvement over the original space, and we are confident that future plans for a permanent, dedicated lactation space as part of the library redesign will continue to foster positive change here at Emory.

Express Yourself
Profiles of Lactation Accommodations

Susan Echols, *library assistant for technical services, Troy University*
Elizabeth Dill, *director of library services, assistant professor, Troy University*

I n March of 2010, the Affordable Care Act (ACA) was signed into federal law. Section 4207 governs that employers must provide reasonable breaks, as well as a private and sanitary area, for most employees needing to "express breastmilk" for their child up to one year after the child is born (United States Breastfeeding Committee, 2018). Even though this law only applies to employees in the workplace, many businesses have been attempting to proactively meet this lactation need for all mothers who use their facilities. A quick Google search will show you that lactation rooms for breastfeeding mothers are on the rise. Such private areas are visible at airports and other public buildings. Libraries are no exception. Many of them have recognized this need as well. While the vast majority of library workers are women—79 percent to be exact (Department for Professional Employees, 2018)—consider how many women commonly visit a public library or special library. How many women go to a school or university or community college and use their libraries on a regular basis? We interviewed librarians at several institutions to get a glimpse of how libraries are providing space for lactation in their facilities.

Cambridge Public Library's Lactation Pod

FIGURE 6.1
Interior photo of Cambridge Public Library's lactation pod
Photo by Maria McCauley

INTERVIEWEE: Maria McCauley, PhD, director of libraries, Cambridge Public Library

Cambridge Public Library director Maria McCauley took notice of the lactation pods at airports. She recalls how when she tried co-working during her holiday break, there were no places to pump. Additionally, she'd had to pump in awkward, unclean, and embarrassing places while traveling for work. Having experienced this firsthand, as these pods became available, she wanted to make sure library patrons could have a clean, private place to pump. Nursing is allowed anywhere in the library, but, of course, parents would have the option of nursing in these pods as well.

Cambridge Public Library's facility manager identified the best location based on space and electrical constraints. Planners also wanted the lactation pod in a space mostly serving adults, so that parents who were co-working and studying could pump. And again, the library supports nursing anywhere in the facility, including the children's floor.

GAINING APPROVAL
Maria and her colleagues discussed the lactation pod plan with City Management, who supported the idea.

COST AND FUNDING
The cost for the ADA lactation pod model was $24,126. The library used a capital project's fund for general improvements.

IMPLEMENTATION
The library considered only ADA models. They needed to make sure they had enough space for these models, which are larger than alternatives. They selected a simple palate (white and maple) to blend in with the Main Library

design (see figure 6.1). City electricians moved existing furniture to other places and installed electric outlets. The library was able to customize the out-of-the-box version. They reduced the product logos, and electricians disabled a built-in reservation by app. Instead, the library established user guidelines and trained public service staff to help promote and manage first-come, first-serve requests. The process of getting set up took about eight months.

> "It makes me grateful to work at a place where women are valued enough to create a dedicated and comfortable space for lactating mothers. The alternative—pumping in a closet (as coworkers did before the mothers' room was created) or under cover at my desk—would have been awkward and uncomfortable and would have created a negative work environment."
>
> —K. Moo, Public Library Digital Services Manager, 2018

OUTCOME

Cambridge Public Library staff and volunteers took pride in being one of the first public libraries in the area to offer this amenity.

Mesa Community College Library's Community Lactation Room

INTERVIEWEE: Ann Tolzman, library department chair, Mesa Community College

During a planned remodeling of the library, staff were looking around and considering the needs. One of Tolzman's colleagues came forward with the idea for a lactation room. The idea had a lot of support, which Tolzman attri-

FIGURE 6.2

Mesa Community College Library's community lactation room

butes to the many women in librarian positions and on campus in general. Many women on campus did not have access to an office to pump in. Students had been seen pumping in bathrooms.

Tolzman and her colleagues identified a book mending room that could be used for lactation. It had a window and a sink and was located next to the refrigerator. (See figure 6.2.)

COST

No costs were incurred.

> "I would have liked a space dedicated to my pumping. I preferred not to pump in the bathroom and used that as a last resort, but I occasionally had no other options. . . . It would also have been nice not to have people knocking on the door when I was pumping."
>
> —K. Shumaker, public library teen librarian, 2018

IMPLEMENTATION

An available room within the library was found and repurposed. Formerly used as a book mending room, it has a sink, a window, and is close to a refrigerator. During implementation, they also researched policies at other institutions because they didn't know if it would be used at all or a lot. And they publicized it.

OUTCOME

Library employees feel that the room is providing a good service, and that it is a good way to drive students to the library.

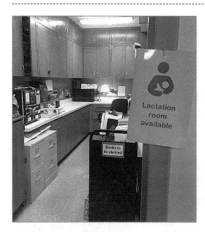

FIGURE 6.3

St. Elmo Elementary School Library's lactation room

St. Elmo Elementary School Library's Lactation Room

INTERVIEWEE: Amy McFadden, school librarian, St. Elmo Elementary School

McFadden needed a private place to pump, and her office in the library worked nicely. It has a door that locks, electric outlets, sink, and a minifridge. A year or two later, a coworker had a baby and McFadden offered her the use of her office if she wanted it. After a couple more teachers requested use, she decided to offer her office as the "official" lactation room.

GAINING APPROVAL

The school principal knew several teachers had used McFadden's office as a lactation room, so when she mentioned making it official, the principal was supportive.

COST

No costs incurred.

> "We don't have room. The idea of me finding somewhere to pump was met with hesitation because we are a very, very small library and there isn't anywhere set up for me to specifically pump."
>
> —Public Library Assistant, 2018

IMPLEMENTATION

Signage (figure 6.3) has been made and staff has been notified about the room. McFadden has also offered to help her teachers by covering their class if they need time to pump. Most make it fit into their regular schedule, but she does occasionally take a class to allow a staff member time to pump, especially when their schedules are disrupted by special meetings or events.

OUTCOME

The teachers who have used it are quite appreciative. However, it's unclear if others notice it.

University of Louisville Law School Library's Lactation Room

INTERVIEWEE: Robin R. Harris, public services librarian and professor of legal bibliography, University of Louisville, Louis D. Brandeis School of Law Library

The President's Commission on the Status of Women (COSW), which Harris chaired during 2002–2003 and 2003–2004, became aware of the need for a lactation room when faculty members contacted COSW members, asking for help in advocating for it.

FIGURE 6.4

University of Louisville Law School Library's lactation room

Photo by Robin R. Harris, Brandeis School of Law Library, University of Louisville

GAINING APPROVAL

The COSW had a direct line to the president and the provost and communicated the idea to them.

FUNDING

No funding was available. The library bore the cost.

IMPLEMENTATION

While this was a campus-wide initiative, the library implementation, several years later, began with the dean of the law school asking the library director to make a room available. The director consulted with a library faculty member (Harris) about room. They made available a room at the back of one of the library's restrooms. (See figure 6.4.)

OUTCOME

No library or law school employees have yet to use the room, but students have.

"It made it a more positive work environment for me because I felt that everyone was understanding. I've heard stories of the horrible 'lactation accommodations' (or lack of) at other workplaces across the country and I find it sad that some employers aren't willing to work with new mothers."

—R. Hooper, Academic Library Head of Reference, 2018

Southern Illinois University–Carbondale, Morris Library's Lactation Room

INTERVIEWEE: Susan Tulis, associate dean of Morris Library

Faculty involved in teaching an architecture class approached the library with a proposed class project. The seminar included two students in architecture,

FIGURE 6.5

Southern Illinois University– Carbondale, Morris Library's lactation room

Image by Susan E. Tulis

> "I was grateful that the university library worked with me. If they hadn't, my experience back would have been more stressful. By supporting my choice to pump, my boss supported my health and the health of my child."
>
> —*Academic Library Assistant, 2018*

two students in construction management, and two in interior design. The three faculty for those units came and said that they wanted to build a lactation room. Tulis was willing to oversee the project and they found space in the library.

GAINING APPROVAL

Tulis was able to say yes or no to the proposed designs, but decisions related to construction were more difficult. Early on, she contacted someone in the physical plant to get them involved. The students could design whatever they wanted, but when it came time to actually construct it, they had to involve workers from the physical plant. Having the physical plant involved early helped to make sure that the designs they came up with were not going to be a problem with connecting electrical work. They did have to move an air vent, and as a union shop it was a little tricky negotiating with the carpenters to let the students do the work. In the end, the students did the work while overseen by the physical plant workers.

COST AND FUNDING

The university puts money toward green fund projects every year. A person working in non-traditional student services may have actually written the grant proposal. The library asked for $20,000 and got $20,000, but only spent $15,177.

IMPLEMENTATION

The major initial roadblock involved convincing the carpenters and the other unionized trade workers to let the students do the work. Tulis had an ally in engineering services who was able to go to the various heads of the trades and convince them. Carpenters and painters didn't do all the work, but they were always there to oversee the project. When aspects of the project were too complicated for the students the tradespeople stepped in. Other than that, everybody else on campus was on board with the idea. Library staff did have some concerns about room security and cleanliness. They discussed how best to allow access to the room, and decided to leave it locked, with key access provided by circulation.

OUTCOME

The lactation room (figure 6.5) definitely made the library look good. It may be unique among lactation rooms on campus for being available for students to use.

References

Department for Professional Employees. (2018, May). Library workers: Facts & figures. Retrieved from http://dpeaflcio.org/programs-publications/issue-fact -sheets/library-workers-facts-figures/

United States Breastfeeding Committee. (2018). Workplace support in federal law. Retrieved from http://www.usbreastfeeding.org/p/cm/ld/fid=200

A Leaf of Faith
Creating Positive, Productive Library Spaces with Plants

Rebecca Tolley, *professor and librarian, East Tennessee State University*

M inor improvements or additions to physical spaces have promising effects upon students' academic performances, as well as library staff and librarians' professional practices and well-being. Bringing living, ornamental plants into our public and private library spaces has immeasurable positive effects upon learning, productivity, efficiency, stress-reduction, pain abatement, noise pollution, and air quality. Rather than viewing plant procurement and placement as a haphazard and individually motivated practice, library administrators and others charged with space assessment and quality improvement should develop formal, organized plans for including a variety of species within all physical spaces inside library buildings.

Living and Ornamental Plants Missing from Library Literature

Information about interior plants and their presence within library spaces is missing from our literature. Articles investigating sustainable and green libraries focus primarily on exterior ecological considerations at the exclusion of interior placement of plants. The Association of College and Research Libraries' (ACRL) online resources describe green buildings and, by extension, the idea of green libraries as "planning design, construction, and operations of buildings with several central, foremost considerations: energy use, water use, indoor environmental quality, material selection and the buildings effect on its site" (LibGuides, n.d.). The majority of information about plants and gar-

dens within these concepts focuses on the outdoors and how libraries' development of "gardens, parks or plazas" extend information literacy services
and programs beyond the physical library space (Rogers, 2017). But there is
nothing within library literature about plantscaping, or the "strategic placement and selection of plant species," which is usually done to engage the eye
and feature architectural details of a building's spatial scheme (Santibanez,
2017). Including indoor plants inside sustainable buildings is a reasonable
assumption, given their effect on indoor air quality (Brilli, 2018). Further, the
topic is missing from literature on space assessment. However, Yang's "Indoor
air pollution and preventions in college libraries" suggests plant placement
within library spaces as a means of improving the indoor environment and
conforming to green building philosophies. With eloquent phrasing, Yang ties
proper plant placement, or function, to aesthetics: "not only can [it] improve
the indoor air quality, but [it] allows readers to feast for the eyes, feeling the
breath of spring" (Yang, 2017). Plants, it seems, are incidental postscripts.

Physical and Psychological Benefits
Gained from Living Plants

Bringing the outdoors inside the library creates inviting, fresh, alive spaces
that may generate positive experiences and lasting impressions. Libraries,
especially academic ones, have a historic reputation for generating library
anxiety in students. Some students feel overwhelmed by the physical space,
but also playing a role are past experiences of library staff attitudes described
as "indifferent, discourteous or even hostile" (Coker, 1993). Plants fill empty
areas and add warmth lacking in institutional architecture that unfortunately
alienates and disengages use of the space. First floors featuring tall ceilings
are more welcoming when tall plants, like ficus trees are added, because they
create a "false ceiling" that changes the eye's perspective and focal point.
Planned plant placement softens institutional edges and makes spaces more
inviting, intimate, and cozier. Interior plants slow down foot traffic in a building, "forcing" people to slow down and relax. Using identical plants in a row
psychologically encourages people to walk quickly through a space, according
to Fediw (Fediw, 2016). Research also shows that people perceive areas dec-
orated with plants to be luxurious and high quality (Wolf, 2002). Seemingly,
library administrators can use plant placement to steer foot traffic toward
service desks, so that students experience less confusion regarding where

they should make face-to-face inquiries, and away from areas where students are prohibited, like staff offices and circulation areas.

Poor indoor air quality control contributes to poor mental and physical health. Adding plants to spaces is a simple and sustainable method for improving air quality, and it also dampens noises. Indoor plants naturally clean indoor air of toxins and chemicals. According to the EPA, Americans spend at least 90 percent of their time indoors (US EPA, n.d.). Indoor air quality often contains more pollutants than outside due to toxic emissions from synthetic building materials, airborne mold, and other pollutants. Plants remove volatile organic compounds (VOCs), such as formaldehyde and benzene, from the air by processing and turning them into energy. Indoor plants reduce carbon monoxide emissions by 90 percent. In spaces where plants are present, people who spend a majority of their time inside buildings experience fewer coughs, sore throats, headaches, and fatigue (Heerwagen, 2012). Indoor plants reduce humidity and dust levels as well. Studies show that people spending time indoors where plants are prevalent have lower blood pressure and feel more attentive and focused on tasks (Lohr, 2010). Plants help buildings regulate the air by stabilizing humidity and temperature, which pays off by reducing energy consumption, thus tying indoor plants more firmly with green or sustainable building theory and practices. Clearly, it seems as though adding living plants to library spaces that are teeming with technology neutralizes stress on people.

Psychical and Psychological Benefits to Library Workers

Adding living plants to public spaces makes the library welcoming to its users. This practice creates a productive place to learn and collaborate. Including plants in faculty and staff offices and workspaces is just as important as arranging them in public spaces. Smith and Pitt suggest that adding plants to workspaces may neutralize or alleviate disengagement and poor performance, which are on the rise amongst office workers worldwide (Smith & Pitt, 2011). They suggest that healthy work environments contribute to staff feelings of well-being (Smith & Pitt, 2009). Shibata and Suzuki discovered that plants in a room dispelled attention fatigue, thus allowing subjects to perform better at tasks with an elevated mood (Shibata & Suzuki, 2004). Beute and de Kort found that exposure to nature, via plants or imagery, had ego-replenishing effects. These are important for exerting self-control and executive function, both instrumental in academic and professional success (Beute & de Kort, 2014). The accumulation of indoor pollutants causes Sick Building Syndrome and Building Related Illnesses. Further, people with multiple chemical sensitivity issues are easily affected by changes in décor such as new carpeting, new flooring, new upholstered and plastic furniture, and other decorative and functional items. Supplementing building spaces with air-purifying plants can neutralize poor environmental conditions that lead to symptoms characteristic of Sick Building Syndrome, including "eye nose and throat irritation; dry skin and mucous membranes; skin rash; mental fatigue; headaches and airway infections; cough; hoarseness, wheezing, itching, hyper-sensitivity; nauseas and dizziness" (Rooley, 1995).

Ornamental Plants Suitable for Library Spaces

According to the National Aeronautics and Space Administration (NASA) Clean Air study, the best air-purifying plants are:

1. Aloe vera, spider plant (*Chlorophytum comosum*)
2. Gerbera daisy (*Gerbera jamesonii*)
3. Snake plant (*Sansevieria trifasciata* "Laurentii")
4. Golden pothos (*Scindapsus aures*)
5. Chrysanthemum (*Chrysantheium morifolium*)
6. Red-edged dracaena (*Dracaena marginata*)
7. Weeping fig (*Ficus benjamina*)
8. Azalea (*Rhododendron simsii*)
9. English ivy (*Hedera helix*)
10. Warneck dracaena (*Dracaena deremensis* "Warneckii")
11. Chinese evergreen (*Aglaonema Crispum* "Deborah")
12. Bamboo palm (*Chamaedorea sefritzii*)
13. Heart leaf philodendron (*Philodendron oxycardium*)
14. Peace lily (*Spathiphyllum*) (Wolverton, Douglas, & Bounds, 1989)

Ficus trees, dracaenas, peace lily, arboricolas, and especially heart-leaf philodendron are effective for noise reduction in instructional and commercial spaces. In addition, bark mulch added to indoor plants' soil surface absorbs sound. Adding dwarf trees or oversized plants to indoor spaces is doable only if they sit atop a rolling slab featuring wheels for easy portability. Guides to plant selection abound on the internet, and it is likely most library collections include books about plants that administrators and space planners may consult. Picking species appropriate for spaces with and without natural lighting is easy, especially when focusing on low-maintenance plants.

Maintenance-Free Living Plants

The majority of plants mentioned above require very little maintenance after the initial investment. Alternatively, ornamental plant procurement may be possible in conjunction with the landscaping and grounds-keeping department within an institution. Academic libraries serving departments of biology, agriculture, forestry, and sustainability may make inquiries about obtaining cuttings and specimens those departments cultivate. Local arboretums, nurseries, and other allied businesses are potential partners, too. Most plant-owning people are amenable to giving cuttings, so another tactic is visiting offices outside the library in search of potential plants. Opportunities for outreach to students exist as well. In collaborating with any of the aforementioned academic departments, the library can highlight plant propagation, cuttings, etc., at appropriate times in the semester and send plant-loving students home with a specimen they can position within their room or dorm, thus transferring the positive psychological effects to their personal space. Each Arbor Day, representatives from our biology department and our campus arboretum hand out Persimmon, Willow Oak, Red Hickory, Sweetbay Magnolia and European hornbeam seedlings. Granted, those are more than most students can commit to, and are not appropriate for cultivating inside academic libraries. Yet, representatives from these units may be amenable to facilitating a plant exchange if student interest compels such actions.

Student workers or volunteers can help with weekly watering tasks. Many cities have plantscaping businesses that allow building administrators to select and add plants to spaces while their staff water, prune, and maintain plants for a monthly fee. Ultimately, this model mimics library trends of access, not ownership, which libraries support through their circulating and digital collections. Hart suggested that removing targets of vandalism, including plants, is the only way to protect them (Hart, 2003). This is a cynical approach and should not discourage plant placement. Keep plants within sight of service desks. In buildings with cameras, monitoring their health is effective remotely. Vandalism in most libraries is incidental and its potentiality should not deter placement of living plants in public spaces.

Conclusion

Most public libraries I have visited displayed philodendron, evergreens, and ficus in public spaces. As a library science student at the University of North Carolina at Greensboro in the mid-1990s, my exposure to academic libraries was limited. One of several strong memories I retain of Jackson Library is that of their plants. They were large, healthy, and well maintained. Several had signs on their containers or sticking out of their soil identifying them by name. Not by scientific name, but by colloquial names that the librarians and staff at Jackson Library gave them. I was hundreds of miles away from home, and that whimsical, caring touch of naming and displaying the plants in areas where I completed assignments created a wealth of positive associations with the library.

Clearly, research supports the inclusion of plants in both public spaces within libraries and in offices and workrooms, where all who spend time working and relaxing inside the building feel their benefits. Anecdotes abound about the positive effect living plants have on people working in academic libraries. Faculty and staff at Charles C. Sherrod Library offer anecdotes concerning the effect plants have on them and on students who visit their offices. Jill Mottern-Stout, cataloging assistant, has a large south-facing window where crown of thorns, philodendron, and rubber trees flourish. She says, "They're inviting" and that "they make you feel good." Joanna Anderson, associate professor and distance education librarian, reports, "Students come in all the time [to my office] and they think it is homey. Ric LaRue, microforms assistant, inherited the largest collection of plants in the library. Microforms are in a public space, on the southwest side of the building, where few students, faculty, or staff venture. In effect, it is a private garden of peace lilies, philodendron, and a red African milk tree that LaRue has pruned several times to prevent it from penetrating the ceiling. Other than private offices and the hidden microforms garden, Sherrod Library lacks natural plants in its public spaces. Undoubtedly, bringing living, ornamental plants into the library space would affect the community that we serve in a positive manner. Readers may view examples of many of species mentioned within this chapter on Instagram via #libraryplants.

References

Association of College & Research Libraries (ACRL). (n.d.). Academic library building design: resources for planning: Green building resources. https://acrl.libguides.com/c.php?g=459032&p=3138052

Beute, F., & de Kort, Y. A. W. (2014). Natural resistance: Exposure to nature and self-regulation, mood, and physiology after ego-depletion. *Journal of Environmental Psychology, 40*, 167–178. https://doi.org/10.1016/j.jenvp.2014.06.004

Brilli, F., Fares, S., Ghirarho, A., de Visser, P., Munoz, A., Annesi-Maesano, I., Sebastinit, F., Alivernini, V., and Menghini, F. (June 2018).Plants for sustainable improvement of indoor air quality. *Trends in Plant Science, 23*(6), 504–512. https://doi.org/10.1016/j.tplants.2018.03.004

Coker, S. (1993). Libraries versus users? How and how not to deter library users. *Library Management, 14*(2), 24. https://doi.org/10.1108/EUM0000000000844

Fediw, K. (2016). What plants contribute to interior design. Timber Press. Retrieved September 27, 2018, from https://www.timberpress.com/blog/2016/05/what-plants-contribute-to-interior-design/

Hart, S. (2003). Vandalism in libraries. Retrieved September 27, 2018, from http://capping.slis.ualberta.ca/cap05/sandy/capping.htm

Heerwagen, J. (2012). The benefits of plants in the workplace. Retrieved September 27, 2018, from https://workdesign.com/2012/07/the-benefits-of-plants-in-the-workplace/

Lohr, V. I. (2010). What are the benefits of plants indoors and why do we respond positively to them? Retrieved from www.actahort.org

Rogers, E. P. (2017). Great outdoor spaces: Library design. *Library Journal.* Retrieved from https://www.libraryjournal.com/?detailStory=great-outdoor-spaces-library-design

Rooley, R. (1995). Sick building syndrome—the real facts—what is known, what can be done. *Structural Survey, 13*(3), 5–8. https://doi.org/10.1108/02630809510099819

Santibanez, D. (2017). What is plantscaping? *Arch Daily.* Retrieved from https://www.archdaily.com/886132/what-is-plantscaping

Shibata, S., & Suzuki, N. (2004). Effects of an indoor plant on creative task performance and mood. *Scandinavian Journal of Psychology, 45*(5), 373–381. https://doi.org/10.1111/j.1467-9450.2004.00419.x

Smith, A., & Pitt, M. (2009). Sustainable workplaces: Improving staff health and well-being using plants. *Journal of Corporate Real Estate, 11*(1), 52–63. https://doi.org/10.1108/14630010910940552

Smith, A., & Pitt, M. (2011). Healthy workplaces: Plantscaping for indoor environmental quality. *Facilities*, *29*(3/4), 169–187. https://doi.org/10.1108/02632771111109289

US EPA, O. (n.d.). The inside story: A guide to indoor air quality. Retrieved from https://www.epa.gov/indoor-air-quality-iaq/inside-story-guide-indoor-air-quality.

Wolf, K. L. (2002). Retail and urban nature: Creating a consumer habitat. Retrieved from http://plantsolutions.com/documents/CreatingAConsumerHabitat.pdf

Wolverton, B. C., Douglas, W. L., & Bounds, K. (1989). A study of interior landscape plants for indoor air pollution abatement. Retrieved from https://ntrs.nasa.gov/search.jsp?R=19930072988

Yang, Z. (2017). Indoor air pollution and preventions in college libraries. *IOP Conference Series: Earth and Environmental Science*, *64*(1), 012076. https://doi.org/10.1088/1755-1315/64/1/012076

In Corpore Sano
Paying Attention to Your Health

Anthony Amodeo, *associate librarian, retired*

I was invited to write this chapter because I had suggested some topics to be included in this book. I had no idea I'd be writing this, but I've witnessed, and in some cases endured, a number of threats to health and well-being over the course of my 38 years working in libraries. Some of these threats, like radiation from the sides and backs of the old CRT computer monitors, are now happily outdated; the final word on microwave radiation, though, is still around the corner.

New knowledge about things like out-gassing of formaldehyde from new furniture, toluene-heavy carpet glues, and "sick building syndrome," which is comprised of several non-specific symptoms, has finally worked its way into the mainstream: however, many threats remain. And, of course, personality weaknesses, from poor management to bullying, are sadly still with us.

Suppression Confession

In many circumstances people tend to be aware of threats to others, but they somehow suppress threat awareness in their own daily work. Sometimes this is deliberate, as in the case of the itinerant "jumpers" at nuclear power plants, who use additional, fake IDs to circumvent the regulated limits on personal exposure time in order to make more money. But many threats are suppressed in one's mind, as the pressures of administrative and personal expectations, deadlines, and just wanting to do a good job tend to make us overlook our own welfare.

I have worked in research and academic libraries, and lived through the transitions from card catalogs, books, print journals and microfilm into our new "digital age." I have participated in disaster recovery and had a strong interest in library preservation throughout my career, from book handling to environmental conditions. Over that time period, I have seen things change—many for the better, but some for the worse. Perhaps I should have spent as much time and energy trying to preserve the health of my peers and myself as preserving library materials.

Inattentiveness as Hazard

All workers are subject to performance and economic pressures, but lower-level employees are often subject to a sometimes surprisingly nineteenth-century style of management and neglect. Libraries might be better places to work than manufacturing plants and warehouses (though they may share some parallel concerns and routines); nevertheless, repetitive movement injuries are something library workers know about, at least by reputation. We all have colleagues, especially among catalogers and webmasters, who developed carpal tunnel problems from the overuse of the keyboard and mouse. However, I was a reference librarian with library instruction and subject acquisitions duties, not the usual cause of overuse or repetitive stress issues. Today, though already retired for three years, whether holding a book, turning a doorknob, or trying to write with a pen or a keyboard, my thumbs remind me that I should have paid more attention to what my body was telling me.

Our new offices came with under-the-desk pull-up keyboards, which could be adjusted a little for height. However, the attached round mousepad did not lie flat, but instead tilted down in front, forcing the wrist to constantly bend upward. I failed to recognize that problem until years later, when, coming to assess another, more serious problem, the ergonomics consultant pointed it out. By then, I had permanently damaged my thumb joint and wrist.

Between preparing for classes (including assignment/subject-focused LibGuides), daily duties, and a lot of consultations with graduate students, both in-person and via email, I often fell behind in ordering books for the several subject areas for which I was responsible. So, as do many, I tried to spend much of the annual allotments late in the season, with only a few weeks before the ordering deadline. I wound up doing much of the book ordering from home at night. Between preparing LibGuides, answering research emails, and book ordering, my nights were very full, and this intense activity did nothing to help my now-complaining thumbs. Again, I wasn't paying attention to the symptoms, wanting to get the work done.

Architects often go for aesthetics over practicality, as many who have worked on a new building or renovation can attest. Our new reference desk was visually beautiful with many features we had asked for. However, the counter was built so high that only barstool-height chairs could be used to access the computer keyboard or see patrons face-to-face. In addition, the counter was built of marble or marble-like stone; beautiful, but unable to be modified easily or aesthetically.

After experiencing almost disabling hip pain every time I worked the desk, I thought I had a hip problem, but nothing seemed to help. Finally, I was diagnosed with a deteriorated spine in the small of my back. I underwent two epidural steroid injections (ESIs), which helped almost immediately. The following day, I happily took my two-hour shift at the reference desk; but by the end of it I was despondent, as the pain returned, worse than before the ESIs.

With my supervisor's cooperation, our institutional ergonomics person first came to my office. Concluding that the tilted mousepad was a problem, we moved the keyboard and mousepad to the top of the desk and adjusted my chair, so that my arm was at the right level. We also readjusted the height of the computer monitor slightly. Moving to the reference desk, she explained that when sitting in a regular chair, much of your weight rests on the floor, but a barstool with your feet on the ring puts all of your weight on the small of your spine. So, every movement, whether bending forward to reach the keyboard or to talk to a patron, or bending sideways to reach for the phone or downwards to get something out of the drawer, puts an enormous twisting strain on your lower spine.

For recovery, I had to work part-time, go on partial state disability, take medicines that made me sleepy, give up bicycling, and change my reference desk setup. I brought in a regular office chair. I stood up to engage with patrons, using interlocking paper box lids to raise the keyboard, and four books to raise the mousepad to a comfortable level for computer use while standing. In what became a permanent adjustment, I used (and carry everywhere) a wedge pillow to take pressure off my spine when sitting, especially in cars and on all but the hardest, flattest chairs.

The dean reacted responsibly, funding adjustable sitting/standing desks for staff; but I'm stuck with my problems and have given up on most of my plans for a productive garden and other physically demanding projects in my retirement. And I still can't comfortably "thumb through" a book or magazine.

The Lesson: Learn to pay attention to your body at the first sign of discomfort and do something about it. Do the homework and consult with an ergonomics expert before designing or reconfiguring workspaces, and especially before construction. Don't let the architects overrule ergonomics with aesthetics. Whether worried about staying productive or just keeping your job, you'll do better for both yourself and your boss if you prevent injuries and health problems.

Disaster Recovery

Years ago, during a long weekend, a fipple (grooved plug) flew off a drip point in an internal plant-watering system, flooding the floor and causing a downstairs "rainstorm." We dealt with sprinkled books in-house, but four boxes of heavily soaked books had to be freeze-dried. Afterwards, I was responsible for inspecting, inventorying and stamping them before they were returned to the shelf. While I and my student worker were sorting through them, we noticed some fibrous powder at the tops of the books; I went home and got a couple of dust masks to keep us from breathing in that powder. I had assumed that it was fiberglass from the ceiling tiles which had been soaked and fallen onto the collection. Only later did I stop to think that it might have been asbestos. Now we know that either substance can lead to future lung problems. I'm glad I thought to get those masks.

The Lesson. When confronted by a disaster, deal first with threats to people, e.g., safe evacuation. Then, deal with prevention of injury to staff, rescuers, recovery personnel, and future users, such as protection from injury due to heavy, wet books, mold, or inhalation of particulate matter, chemicals, etc., during and after recovery. Informed and commonsense plans for the worst-case scenarios are a must. Practice and follow the plan, and you'll come out of it better.

New Acquisitions

Decades ago, a research library I worked for received a very large and valuable collection of materials from the estate of the widow of a famous writer. In the large wooden bins, there were manuscripts galore, books, newspaper clippings, pencils, desk decorations, and a lot of unrelated personal items, including, somehow, pairs of used pantyhose. Acquisitions librarians and rare book librarians know that donations aren't always in good shape. And sometimes they can be a threat, whether from mold or insect infestation. At another library I worked for, new book additions were routinely fumigated before being added to the collections, using a fumigation chamber large enough to hold a book truck. But having this chamber in the library presented a health hazard, so very strict procedures had to be implemented, including adequate post-fumigation ventilation of materials before human contact.

The Lesson: Whether for sanitary reasons, dust, mold or insect infestations, donations should be examined and handled with care before being integrated into the collections, both for the sake of staff and the protection of the collections. Undertake remedial measures with informed and detailed planning and great care. Have a list of professional consultants and services at hand.

Environmental Concerns

Like all buildings, libraries are subject to environmental problems, such as dust and mold and poor ventilation, including around 3D printers. Construction almost always introduces additional complications, sometimes including risks of fire or flood. At one library, new handrails were being spray-varnished in-house after installation and the fumes affected the staff. At another library, I joined a conversation between the library's head and the carpeting contractor, asking if the glue they were about to use was one of the heavy-toluene glues in common use. I spoke of people sensitive to chemicals not being able to use the library, probably for months, if that glue was used. The better glue increased costs, so only one floor was done that year instead of two. But "access to information" wasn't curtailed, and no one got sick.

On a Saturday morning, responding to an ant infestation, an exterminator sprayed our closed building under the direction of the head of the library. He remained with the exterminator, yet both failed to take into account that the library head wasn't wearing a mask, as the exterminator was. The head librarian wound up spending the rest of the weekend in the hospital.

The Lesson: Insect poisons, volatile organic compounds (VOCs), and all the things that create sick building syndrome add up to threats to health for at least some employees and patrons. Any changes, additions, repairs, etc., need to be examined in detail with prior consultation on possible environ-mental effects with outside contractors—*every time*. Pregnant women, of course, need to be especially aware of possible contaminations, and avoid them entirely. As for daycare facilities, children's growing brains and bodies are affected by all kinds of toxins—including chemical scents and perfumes.

Finally

You know, in the back of your mind, that sometimes you ignore your body at work. You know you need to get up every 20 minutes or so and move around. You know that, when on the computer, you need to look at faraway objects for at least ten minutes per hour, to keep your eye muscles from getting messed up. You know you should not wait 20 minutes to use the bathroom when you need to! But you know all too well that you often ignore what's good for you. Change that behavior. You won't regret it. Pay attention to your body and learn and stick to the ergonomic guidelines we all hear. . . and often ignore. You'll be a more productive employee over time, and you'll enjoy your work and your life.

All work involves some level of stress, from creative stress before an accom-plishment to the kinds of emotional stress that do harm. Excess stress and lack of sleep are known disease breeders, from nervous disorders to diabetes. Get your seven hours a night; read those articles about off-device relaxation, darkness, and other strategies if you have trouble dropping off at night—or if you're having no trouble dropping off during the day!

And, please, support colleagues who are harassed or bullied. Support your colleagues who are under threats to health, especially by outside services that get more respect because they are getting paid to do a job. So are you! And your colleagues! And your illness will affect your workplace far more than making the outside contractor adhere to sensible guidelines. Be willing to do research for articles, published data, and other evidence regarding any partic-ular threat, if that is what's needed to convince your boss. These days, given OSHA, the ADA, and other guidelines, it shouldn't be as hard as it used to be, despite recent reversals and science denial by certain government agency heads. Better that sometimes-uncomfortable ounce of prevention than a life-time of trying to cure what can't be cured. Stay well.

Further Reading

How work kills us. *Economist*. Retrieved from https://www.economist.com/open-future/2018/07/18/how-work-kills-us

National Institutes of Health. (2018). *TOXNET*. https://toxnet.nlm.nih.gov/

Pfeffer, Jeffrey. (2018). *Dying for a paycheck: How modern management harms employee health and company performance—And what we can do about it.* New York, NY: HarperCollins.

The California Preservation Program (CPP) (2018). Retrieved from https://calpreservation.org/.

Typing? Check your sitting posture. (2018). WebMD Retrieved from https://www.webmd.com/back-pain/typing-posture-pain-prevention#1

Benefits of Employee Exercise and the Impact on Mental Health

Kayla Kuni, *librarian, Pasco-Hernando State College (FL)*

Exercise can be a wonderful way to help a person feel good about themselves, all while getting some much-needed physical activity in a field that, let's be honest, isn't that strenuous. When I worked in technical services, and agreed to help cover a children's storytime, I realized how out of shape I truly was. I felt bad after storytime was over and like I had let the kids down. They were used to a high-energy librarian . . . and that day they got *me*. My poor physical health impacted my self-worth that day and made me reevaluate what I was doing with my diet and what I was doing to myself with such criticism. My poor physical performance led me to an emotional place that I was not prepared for at the time, but I have come to find it may have saved my life.

The relationship between mental health and exercise is something that has been discussed over the years. It has even been found that a withdrawal from exercise has deleterious effects. According to Weinstein, Koehmstedt, and Kop (2017), "Exercise withdrawal consistently resulted in increases in depressive symptoms and anxiety." One would not necessarily treat an employee that is having a bad day in the same manner that one would treat an employee who is experiencing depression. "An estimated 6 to 7 percent of full-time workers in the United States live with major depression" (Greenberg, 2018). Depressed employees "miss an average of 31.4 workdays each year and lose another 27.9 workdays to unproductivity—or presenteeism—which costs employers an estimated $44 billion annually" (Greenberg, 2018). As a manager, one may recognize some symptoms of depression, such as: "Difficulty concentrating, remembering or making decisions," "Increased errors and diminished work quality," "Procrastination and missed deadlines," "Withdrawal from co-workers," "Decreased interest in work," and the aforementioned attendance issues (Baldelomar, 2018). It is clearly a benefit for organizations to be concerned about the mental health of their employees as it relates to potential organizational losses. One such solution to helping employees feel mentally well is to offer an employee exercise program or some kind of incentive for employees to be active.

A library should not have issues in convincing stakeholders that implementing exercise programs at work is a good idea. We know that exercise has an impact on depression, but not all employees are necessarily ready to adopt exercise at the time that the organization rolls out the opportunities. It is important for managers to be well versed in the topic of depression. According to Crist (2018), when managers are supportive and speak about the topic of depression, "absenteeism is lower, and presenteeism is higher." We want our teams to come to work, but we want them to be engaged and feel that they are making an impact. In order to achieve better ends for both absenteeism and presenteeism, we must consider the impact that being relatively sedentary has on our teams. For those of us that sit at a desk most of our day, it is not only important to get up and move for our own health, but also for our productivity at work. From the business management perspective, the cost savings from absenteeism and other health-care related costs will benefit the organization; however, these cost saving measures may also have a positive impact upon the individual employees and their well-being. Employees need to feel valued at their place of employment, and nothing will make them feel more important than knowing their employer cares about their health.

My experience at storytime several years ago led me to reevaluate how I was taking care of myself, in several capacities. I was in poor physical health and that physical health was impacting my mental health. I felt bad about myself because, on the surface, I was letting the kids down with a low-energy storytime; beneath the surface, I was emotionally exhausted, eating food that was bad for me, and that was further contributing to my poor self-esteem. The decision to get healthy is indeed a personal choice. No one can be forced to get physical, no matter how often you pump the Olivia Newton-John song through your computer speakers. The decision to get healthy will be up to individual choice; however, institutions can help to provide a place for ideas, support, and incentives (without turning healthy goals into a competition). I have made choices that have had a positive impact on my future, largely due to the opportunities I had during my time with the City of New Port Richey. Institutional access to a gym, something I did not have the financial means to pay for myself at the time, allowed me to start a routine that I was able to carry with me in my future career.

Walking Meetings

We should start by looking at what can be done, what should be done, and why those things aren't already being done now. For example, one day my provost walked into the library in shorts and a T-shirt. I commented on how comfortable her sneakers looked and she explained to me that she and our dean had walking meetings. Walking meetings were beneficial to the two main administrators on my campus because (1) it was healthy, (2) meetings in offices can waste electricity, and (3) it is good to be seen modeling healthy behaviors to the students. One of the benefits of a walking meeting is that "the act of walking leads to increases in creative thinking" (Clayton, Thomas, & Smothers, 2015). In addition to being a low-cost option for employers, these meetings tend to lead to high employee engagement. A friend of mine participated in her office's walking lunch session in order to lose weight; the employee who lost the most weight won some coveted prize. While rewarding good behavior is not a bad thing, the competitive element for weight loss can be problematic. Anyone remember *The Biggest Loser*? Many of the folks on that show ended up gaining their weight back after production wrapped and then had to deal with the shame of accomplishing a goal but then failing miserably on a national stage (Brodwin, 2017). Instead of turning health initiatives into a competition, consider turning them into a hybrid of professional development opportunities and relationship building between staffers and themselves.

Health Club Benefit

When I first started working for the City of New Port Richey, FL, I was told that one additional benefit I had was free access to the city's state of the art recreation and aquatic facility. I took advantage of my membership a few times, either before work or during lunch. In my course of employment with the city I encountered several of my peers who had no idea that we had this gym perk. Now, maybe the city did not do a great job of promoting this benefit to new hires, or maybe they forgot. Either way, a few years ago there was a *The Biggest Loser*-style program that was open to city employees. While I am not a fan of the show the program was based on, I participated and found that it was consistent with my gym behavior when I had a goal in mind. I met a lot of new colleagues from other departments; these are people that I had never met before and likely never would have met aside from this workout program. While we were "competing" against one another, we could also support one another in our goals. For a few of us, weight loss was not our main goal, even though it was the intent of the program. My primary goal was to establish a routine and feel good about myself.

Make It Fun

Exercise is great for keeping one motivated, but some caution needs to be expressed when advocating for exercise programs, particularly as they relate to mental health. We have likely all heard of cheat days, or days when we eat junk food or skip our gym workouts. For some people, cheat days are not a big deal; they get back on the program the following day. For others, though, cheat days can lead to a day of self-loathing and contempt. As leaders, it is important to support staff in whatever kind of physical program gets incorporated into the organization, and to also surveil the program and keep an eye out for harmful impacts. Exercise programs should be fun, and increase productivity and the sharing of good ideas. If the program is not leading to positive feelings among your team, you might need to reconsider the program and redevelop it with more staff input. Remember, the best type of exercise is the kind that doesn't feel like exercise. Give your team ideas as to what kind of physical games they can partake in. My college has an annual staff vs. students flag football game in the fall. The physical practicing that is done before such an event leads to better team building, more confidence, and better communication skills with colleagues.

All organizations are different, and all governing bodies react differently to new ideas. The concept of walking meetings might face very little opposition in one organization while failing miserably in another. Each librarian knows their team, their administration, and exactly how difficult something like exercise programs at work will be to implement. The purpose of these types of programs is to increase employee engagement, increase employee mental health, and increase employee physical health. The priority should not be placed on a physical transformation with these programs; the focus is on engagement and mental well-being. If employees end up losing weight, that is a great added benefit. At the end of the day, the goal is to have employees feeling good about themselves, their career, and their contribution to the team.

References

Baldelomar, R. (January 31, 2018). Focus on wellness: How to help employees cope with depression at work. *Forbes*. Retrieved from https://www.forbes .com/sites/raquelbaldelomar/2018/01/31/focus-on-wellness-how-to-help -employees-cope-with-depression-at-work/ #6d7ad2a842a0

Brodwin, E. (June 11, 2017). A new show features "Biggest Loser" winners who regained weight—and reveals a deeper truth about weight loss. *Business Insider*. Retrieved from https://www.businessinsider.com/new-show-biggest -loser-winners-regained-weight-big-fat-truth-2017-6

Clayton, R., Thomas, C., & Smothers, J. (2015). How to do walking meetings right. *Harvard Business Review Digital Articles*, 2–4. Retrieved from http:// ezproxy.lib.usf.edu/login?url=http://search.ebscohost.com/login.aspx ?direct=true&db=buh&AN=118667251&site=eds-live

Crist, C. (August 10, 2018). Manager support of employees with depression may reduce absenteeism. *Reuters*. Retrieved from https://www.reuters.com/ article/us-health-workplace-depression/manager-support-of-employees -with-depression-may-reduce-absenteeism-idUSKBN1KV1YB

Greenberg, R. (July 31, 2018). Depression calculator tallies business costs of employees' mental illness. Retrieved from https://psychnews.psychiatry online.org/doi/10.1176/appi.pn.2018.8a7

Weinstein, A. A., Koehmstedt, C., & Kop, W. J. (2017). Review article: Mental health consequences of exercise withdrawal: A systematic review. *General Hospital Psychiatry*, *49*, 11–18. https://doi-org.ezproxy.lib.usf.edu/10.1016/ j.genhosppsych.2017.06.001

10

Walk and Learn for Wellness

Kelsey Brett, *head of discovery and metadata department, University of Colorado–Denver*
Melody Condron, *resource description and management coordinator, University of Houston*
Lisa Martin, *coordinator of outreach, University of Houston*

Walk and Learn for Wellness

A small team at the University of Houston (UH) Libraries was awarded an internal grant to implement a library employee wellness program. The program, dubbed Walk and Learn for Wellness, consisted of three parts: a walking challenge in fall, a series of lunch and learn workshops in spring, and the purchase of a treadmill desk for general use during and after the end of the grant period. Objectives of the program included increasing overall awareness of wellness in library employees, providing basic information about health and wellness to employees, and connecting employees to existing wellness resources. Attendees expressed enthusiasm for the program and a survey showed measurable gains in awareness on wellness topics. Although the program was funded through a small grant (primarily used to purchase the treadmill desk), similar models could be used at other libraries at no or low cost while still providing benefit for employees.

Perspectives and Advice

At-work wellness programs have been recognized repeatedly as a way to engage a workforce and improve the health and well-being of employees through preventative and proactive care (Oluwaseyi et al., 2017). There are many benefits to an employer when employees are healthier, including workers missing fewer days, paying lower insurance premiums, and creating more engaged teams. For employees, wellness programs offer ways to improve their lives: lower stress, better health, and (sometimes) a better team dynamic with coworkers. Such programs indicate to employees that their well-being is valued, and employees may experience higher morale/greater "buy-in" on the job (Abdullah & Lee, 2012).

Every wellness program is different, and each program depends on the amount of energy, space, and time that a library has to contribute to it.

Library wellness programs might include

- designated exercise space and equipment in the library,
- standing or treadmill desks, for shared or personal in-office use,
- library programs for staff that encourage healthy living (such as seminars on healthy eating or meditation),
- walking/activity challenges or planned daily walks,
- free on-site health screenings,
- incentives for healthy activity participation (such as going for a check-up or attending health-focused classes), and
- incentives and/or encouragement of supervisors to adopt healthy habits, such as walking meetings. Supervisors may also need help understanding why their team should be able to participate in wellness activities during work time.

Gaining Administrative Support

Lisa German, dean of libraries at the University of Houston, shared these thoughts on wellness initiatives: "The wellness of library employees should be of preeminent concern. Good wellness programs improve the health of both the body and mind of our employees, which, in turn, affects their work in a positive way. A wellness [initiative] can be a recruitment/retention incentive for a library organization because it shows that the library administration cares about the whole of our employees and not just their work."

Gaining administrative support for health and wellness initiatives in libraries should not be difficult. Library leaders are generally receptive to initiatives that have been proven successful through research and data analysis, as wellness initiatives have been. Share that research with decision makers and participants to gain support as you plan.

Library teams interested in making their case should provide a clearly outlined plan to their administration. A plan should include the following: what will be done; timing (set period or ongoing); who will manage the initiatives; what is expected from administration; any budgetary needs or concerns; and desired outcomes (what will be gained). In addition, most library leaders are receptive to initiatives that clearly tie into a library's goals or strategic plans in a meaningful way.

One possible concern is loss of productivity. However, in a study by Koepp, et al. (2013), researchers concluded that office workers improved their health without affecting work performance when they had access to treadmill desks at work. The key is to make sure that wellness initiatives are supported by administration and managers who know what the expected benefits will be.

Specific Steps Taken

University of Houston Libraries offers a micro-grant program to spur internal innovation through small grants of under $2,000 awarded for projects "in support of UH Libraries' Strategic Directions and the University's Tier One initiatives" (UH Libraries, n.d.). The project team was awarded a micro-grant of $1,836 for a yearlong project covering a fall walking challenge, a spring lunch and learn workshop series, and a treadmill desk. The grant purchased a treadmill desk (around $1,600) as well as pedometers (around $250) for the walking challenge participants.

The walking challenge was held in the fall and enrolled over 50 percent of library staff. The project team used Walk Across Texas, which is a free eight-week program for tracking exercise entered by participants. The site, not limited to Texans, handles registration and tracking and provides support.

The walking challenge kicked off in September with an event where pedometers were handed out and the libraries' dean spoke. During the eight weeks of the challenge, the project team sent weekly emails to participants to encourage logging of exercise and participant retention, both of which were reinforced by a midpoint event to rally teams. The challenge ended in December with a closing celebration where participants were recognized and provided healthy snacks to enjoy (sponsored by campus dining services).

The treadmill desk was delivered in September. Library staff, including participants in the walking challenge, were encouraged to use the desk by checking out the access key to its private room. Use was tracked through ILS reports and a sign-in clipboard.

In the spring, the project team held four "Lunch and Learn" sessions to promote wellness across the library. These were held in January (self-care in the new year), February (nutrition and healthy grocery shopping), March (stress and work-life balance) and April (cancer prevention and healthy well-being). Speakers for the lunch and learn sessions were recruited from various campus departments at no cost.

Project members surveyed library staff in the fall and spring in order to have pre- and post-assessments that addressed the project objectives (particularly the objective to increase overall awareness of wellness). Fifty-one percent of responding staff members indicated that they had used the treadmill desk or intended to do so, a majority attended at least one spring lunch and learn session, and overall staff interest in exercise and other areas of wellness increased.

Solutions to Possible Roadblocks

Employee wellness programs are so adjustable that almost any roadblock can be overcome; nevertheless, there are some challenges that should be anticipated and planned for as an institution starts a new program.

Participation is key for a successful wellness program, and oftentimes that requires some kind of motivation. In a voluntary employee wellness program, rewards, rather than penalties, are the best option. We found that the competitive nature of the walking challenge offered a fun and positive motivation to participate. Having an ongoing reward system may encourage regular participation. This could be as simple as sending out an email to recognize participation or offering a small prize to the individual or group that completes or wins a monthly challenge. While the walking competition served as a motivator for some, it was a roadblock for others who were uncomfortable with competition. Depending on the culture of a workplace, the level of competition can easily be adjusted. We adjusted our original plan, to recognize individual as well as group winners, and to only recognize group accomplishments. To incentivize participation, everyone who signed up received an inexpensive pedometer, and to reward participation, everyone was invited to enjoy the award ceremony.

Offering the wellness program on a voluntary basis is also key to a successful implementation. Not all individuals are comfortable discussing health and wellness or participating in a competition that requires certain physical abilities. Everyone should feel free to participate, or not, in ways that make them feel comfortable. In our case, each aspect of the wellness program was offered individually. For example, an employee could use the walking desk and attend the lunch and learns but choose not to participate in the walking challenge. Be mindful of including people with varying levels of ability. The walking challenge we adopted included a calculator that converted a wide variety of exercises and physical activity, from powerlifting to gardening, into miles walked. This allowed us to have an inclusive walking challenge that did not necessarily require a specific physical ability.

Some employees hesitated to participate because they did not feel empowered to take walking breaks or leave their desks for extended periods of time to use the walking desk as they worked, even though that is exactly what the desk was intended for. Ongoing and explicit supervisory support and encouragement is essential for making employees feel comfortable in participating, especially if this type of activity was not encouraged in the past. This is why it is so important to have administrative support for your wellness program from the beginning. Reminders about wellness offerings and affirmations aimed at those who take advantage of them from administration and supervisors can contribute to developing a workplace culture that encourages physical activity throughout the day.

Monetary constraints are oftentimes roadblocks to implementing a new program. While the employee wellness program at UH Libraries did require some funding, much of the program could have been completed without any money at all. While an investment of staff time was needed to implement the wellness program, as long as administration approves of employees spending part of their time developing and administering a wellness program, it can be done at little to no cost. If you do have funds, you can spend them on something like a treadmill desk, although it is not necessary to do so. Once we identified a space for the walking desk, people from the library started donating other exercise equipment for the room, such as yoga mats and free weights. You can have a donation drive for fitness equipment and make a small collection of second-hand products available. You could also promote equipment-free exercise ideas, such as office chair yoga. We also spent some of our funds on incentives for participation, such as the UH Libraries branded pedometers, but they were not essential to the success of the program.

Recognition of Future Staff Needs

The UH Libraries employee wellness program was developed by a group of volunteers in the library. While the first year of the wellness program may require the largest time investment, successful wellness programs do require long-term staff support. In UH Libraries' case, the project volunteers were not able to incorporate employee wellness into their job duties on an ongoing basis. For a successful, long-term employee wellness program, people need to be responsible for it. There are multiple ways that this can be addressed. One or more employees can have wellness responsibilities added to their job description and given the time and support to attend to those responsibilities. Another approach would be to form a wellness committee and have staff rotate on and off, so that they only have wellness responsibilities for a specified period of time.

Wellness programs are often available to your employees outside of your internal organization. Look for opportunities in your community, whether it be your university, city, county, or school district, for wellness programs that are already in place. While the UH Libraries was implementing their wellness program, the University of Houston hired its first Wellness and Engagement Administrator, who was tasked with developing a campus-wide wellness program. After the Libraries' initial employee wellness project ended, it relied on programming and activities developed at the campus level to satisfy the wellness needs of employees. This still required internal support to promote and encourage employees to participate, but it required a far smaller time commitment than running an internal wellness program year after year.

Conclusion

With multiple possible benefits to wellness programs, libraries seeking to engage and energize their employees should consider implementing health and wellness initiatives. Budgets large and small can be adapted to meet local needs, and library administration can usually be brought on board with good research and data analysis results and the desire for healthier, happier employees.

References

Abdullah, D. N. M. A., and Lee, O. Y. (2012). Effects of wellness programs on job satisfaction, stress and absenteeism between two groups of employees (attended and not attended). *Procedia - Social and Behavioral Sciences, 65,* 479-484. doi: 10.1016/j.sbspro.2012.11.152

Koepp, G. A., Manohar, C. U., McCrady-Spitzer, S. K., Ben-Ner, A., Hamann, D. J., Runge, C. F. & Levine, J. A. (2013). Treadmill desks: A 1-year prospective trial. *Obesity, 21,* 705-711. doi:10.1002/oby.20121

Oluwaseyi O. Isehunwa, Erik L. Carlton, Yang Wang, Yu Jiang, Satish Kedia, Cyril F. Chang, Daniel Fijabi, & Soumitra S. Bhuyan (2017). Access to employee wellness programs and use of preventive care services among U.S. adults. *American Journal of Preventive Medicine, 53*(6), 54-865. doi: 10.1016/j.amepre.2017.08.001

University of Houston Libraries. (n.d.). Microgrant Committee. Retrieved from http://intranet.lib.uh.edu/microgrant

11

OM Nom Nom
Integrating Yoga with Your Lunch Break

Patricia M. Dragon, *head of special cataloging, East Carolina University*
Katy Webb, *head of research and instructional services, East Carolina University*
Rebecca Tatterson, *electronic resources librarian, East Carolina University*

Yoga is a practice that was developed in India starting about 5,000 years ago. Its popularity has increased in the United States in recent decades, with many specialized studios, gyms, community centers, and other organizations offering yoga classes. At East Carolina University's Joyner Library, a small group of staff who had experience with yoga from these other venues decided to form a lunchtime yoga group in the library. We get together at noon most Tuesdays and Thursdays, go into a free classroom, and do yoga for about 30 minutes. We do not have a leader, but rather follow yoga videos on screens in the classroom. The members of our group have changed over a period of years, and we have gone through busy phases during which we have not met regularly, but the group persists because we derive benefits from it.

The Benefits of Yoga and Mindfulness

While the physical component of yoga is probably the one most Westerners are familiar with, yoga actually integrates physical, mental, and spiritual components, and conveys health benefits in all these areas. In the workplace we focus on the first two areas, physical and mental. On the physical side, yoga emphasizes stretching, core strength, and above all, breathing. Stretching can counteract the effects of sitting down most of the day at a computer, including tight hamstrings, repetitive muscle stress, and neck pain. Developing core

71

strength can help prevent and relieve back pain, and mindful breathing can fight poor circulation and digestive problems. Contrary to the impressions some have of yoga, the goal is not to compete to see who can most convincingly bend oneself into a pretzel. There are many styles and adaptations, including gentle yoga designed for seniors, and desk yoga designed to be done sitting while in work clothes. It is a good workplace activity because it truly is possible for almost anyone to do it.

Yoga also has mental health benefits. It is typically practiced in a quiet, dark room, which is a pleasant break from the library noise and activity (yes, there is a lot of noise in the library), as well as the glare of computer screens. The practice of moving with your breath and focusing your attention on its rhythms is an antidote to the multitasking we all do on a daily basis. While it is no substitute for medical care, yoga really can counteract stress and make you feel better. We have even found it to be good for organizational health by promoting team dynamics and increasing communication opportunities across departments. Rarely a yoga session goes by without several of us collaborating on work problems as we turn on the lights and roll up the mats.

History of Joyner Yogis

The yoga group at Joyner Library developed because interested members wanted to establish a regular yoga practice on or near campus. In 2013, a library employee took yoga teacher training and started offering the first yoga sessions in the library to meet a quota of hours for her certification. Tables and chairs were cleared from a large meeting room and the sessions lasted for one hour. Although the employee left the library soon after, the core group for the yoga time was formed out of these sessions.

The Joyner Yogis hoped to find a way to continue their practice despite the loss of the librarian/yoga instructor, and in 2014 and 2015, the Campus Recreation and Wellness Center (CRW) offered free lunchtime yoga sessions on Tuesdays. These were aimed at an audience of students and were taught by one of the counselors at the Counseling Center. She allowed university staff to attend the hour-long sessions to reduce workplace stress. Drawbacks were that this was just one time per week and the sessions' availability waxed and waned with the semesters. The room was not available on weeks where the yoga instructor was not present and there was a convoluted sign-up process. A paid option for yoga one evening after work per week was soon available through the CRW. The instructor was very engaging, but soon left to start her own yoga studio in mid-2015. Like the lunch yoga sessions, this option was only available one day per week and was not available during semester breaks and over the summer.

The Joyner Yogis group started in earnest in mid-2015 and grew out of a larger library initiative to promote teamwork and inter-departmental coop-eration. This larger initiative set a number of other lunchtime activities into motion, such as a book club, a knitting club, a puzzle group, and a walking group. Upon their inception, the Yogis decided to meet on Tuesdays and Thurs-days at lunchtime, since there was an aerobics class available at the CRW on Monday, Wednesday, and Friday at lunchtime. This would allow those inter-ested to have a workout every day of the week over the noon hour. Since there are no longer any employees able to serve as a yoga teacher, videos and iPad applications have been used during these sessions. Besides a semester-long hiatus in fall 2017 that coincided with a participant's maternity leave, the Joyner Yogis have been meeting in a library classroom for over three years.

What Is Needed?

After determining an approximate size of your group, locating a comfortable location that is large enough to accommodate the group is essential. Joyner Library has several large meeting rooms available for use, so one of the par-ticipants will usually determine an available room to reserve for the session. Room availability can vary during the times of year when instruction is busi-est. Occasionally a room is not available, and on those occasions the group is unable to meet.

In the absence of an instructor, we have found that many online yoga vid-eos are a worthy substitute. If using a yoga video for instruction, the practice space will need either a screen to project the video session or an internet con-nection to accommodate broadcast from an iPad or laptop. Joyner Yogis have a few favorites that are included in this chapter.

Aside from the essentials—a space to practice and an instructor or the equivalent in the form of a video or DVD—there are a few supplemental items that can be helpful. A yoga mat provides a comfortable, safe surface to prac-tice and is highly recommended. Occasionally, props are utilized in instruc-tion videos and sessions; however, oftentimes our group manages without them and can still perform the poses. A change of clothes is recommended as it can help with comfort. Many yoga poses require extensive movement and stretching, and even laying or sitting on the floor, so comfortable clothing allows for this kind of movement.

Group Rules and Guidelines

The group is open to anyone who would like to join in. We invite participation, usually by word of mouth. Many new employees have joined in after telling one of the Yogis that they like to practice yoga outside of work. We are not professional yoga instructors, and none of us serve as the instructor, which means we cannot check for proper form or even give each other guidance during the sessions. (In fact, the room is dark, so we often do not even look at each other at all.) For that reason, the Joyner Yogis require that new recruits to our group have some prior yoga experience. For those who have no prior yoga experience but who want to join in, we recommend starting with a yoga basics session through a local yoga studio.

The Joyner Yogis have an email list of people who have been involved in the group recently, as well as a calendar item that shows up on individual Outlook calendars. Group participation is very flexible, and people can join in when they are able. Each Tuesday and Thursday, an email is sent to the group to see if practice that day will be possible. This is based on room availability and the presence of the people in the group, which we check the day of.

Some guidelines that we follow in our group are that our yoga practice is not about performance or even form. It is a personal practice for each person in the room. If we are doing a video where there is something that an individual cannot do, we do not expect them to do it or push themselves to get there. Our practice space is a no judgment zone.

Yoga Websites and Apps

Anyone who has practiced yoga knows that new products are coming out by the day. The main locations that you will find yoga videos are on websites, iTunes applications, YouTube channels, or through readily available subscription services like Amazon Prime. While the group continuously discusses and evaluates video resources, some of our favorite websites and applications (at the time of this book's publication) are listed on the following page.

Do Yoga with Me, standalone website: https://www.doyogawithme.com/
This site offers free and paid options for high-quality yoga videos. The instructors are from British Columbia, Canada. Joyner Yogis recommend the videos by David Procyshyn, one of the founders. A positive feature on this site is that it is easily searchable by instructor, style of yoga, level of difficulty, and amount of time you have to practice.

Yoga with Adriene, YouTube Channel: https://www.youtube.com/user/yogawithadriene
Adriene is a cartoon voice actress with an engaging demeanor and sense of humor. The videos are high quality and there are a lot of them to choose from. Her adorable dog, Benji, makes regular appearances.

Yoga Studio app, iTunes application: http://www.yogastudioapp.com/
This application was a favorite at the beginning of our group's existence. We especially liked the calming music loops and backgrounds. It is recommended for iPad or iPhone users, but there is a nominal cost associated with it.

There are many benefits to be derived from incorporating regular exercise into one's daily routine. Several members of Joyner Yogis briefly explain how our practice enhances their workday. A new member to the group said, "As a new employee in a new town, I was delighted to learn about the informal lunchtime yoga that happens here in the library. The sessions are just the right length to restore balance to my mind and body while still allowing me to grab a quick bite to eat. Best of all, I now have a fabulous group of new work-friends!" Others mentioned the benefits of staying limber, releasing tension, and seeing coworkers that we do not normally see during the day. The important thing is to have fun and provide a relaxing environment that allows camaraderie and a social opportunity for employees.

Reference

Morrison, V. (June 2013). Yoga benefits the body and mind. *Occupational Health, 65*(6), 27–29.

A Call for Sensitivity toward Race and Ethnicity

Angel Sloss, *digital reference and embedded librarian, Tennessee State University*

D uring my short years as a professional librarian and manager, there has always been a consensus that there aren't enough library personnel from various cultures in the field. Discussions have turned to how to recruit and promote persons of color, but what I have noticed is that little has been done to retain and promote minorities currently in the field. How do we recruit more people into the profession if we are not giving them job growth and stability like their majority counterparts? The answer is not simple, but we can work towards the right path by integrating discussions of race, ethnicity, inclusion, and sensitivity into our workplaces.

Libraries must do more to ensure that all personnel of varied racial backgrounds have chances to voice their concerns and their stories, and that they feel welcomed to do so. In a society where persons of color are often made to feel inferior, sharing concerns isn't always easy. Persons of color need to feel confident that they can share what makes them feel unwelcome or uneasy in the workplace with their peers. While people of color succeed in society, they often must assimilate to societal norms or alter pieces of their personality that may be attributed to their culture or race to achieve the same level of success as their counterparts.

Library Worker Demographics

I was unaware of the racial divisiveness that existed within the library field. Many scholarly articles discuss the implications of having more females enter the profession than male and what those outcomes would look like in the future. The Department for Professional Employees compiled a 2018 fact sheet entitled, "Library Workers: Facts & Figures." With regards to diversity among library workers, however, the library profession has failed to show an increase in racial and ethnic diversity and there are few signs that this is improving. Over 86 percent of librarians were white, non-Hispanic in 2017; however, library technicians had greater diversity.

Among library assistants in 2017, just over 80 percent were white, non-Hispanic. In 2017, just 6.4 percent of librarians were of African American descent, 10.4 percent were Hispanic or Latino, and only 5.2 percent were Asian. Overall, among all workers in education, training and library professions, African Americans only made up 10 percent of the field, while Hispanic and Asian professionals represented 10 percent and 4.7 percent of the education workforce. I realized that I would represent a smaller minority of African American female professionals entering the field (for African American men, even smaller). The chances that I would see or interact with library professionals of Native American, Latino, and Asian descent would be bleak.

Microaggressions

I always thought that I would be entering a profession that would largely embrace my love for reading and researching, but I was mistaken. I was not prepared for the constant microaggressions that I would feel in the workplace. Microaggressions are generally described as racially or culturally insensitive, passive-aggressive behaviors that are subtle to those who are less experienced in its totality. For example, being dismissive or not eliciting sympathy for a colleague who feels discriminated against or feeling uncomfortable with questions about skin-tone, race, or culture. Many people may view such questions as "natural curiosity," but it becomes offensive when it borderlines on racial stereotypes. So how do we identify and resolve microaggressive behavior? We can identify microaggressive behavior in diversity and inclusion training. To break down the walls that microaggression creates within the profession and advance, the profession (from a HR viewpoint) should identify the root of offensive behaviors. Behaviors that contribute to the stereotyping and/or mistreatment of those from different ethnicities are rooted in fear and lack of knowledge for diversity.

Exploring ways that bias occurs in race/culture, defining microaggressions and producing training products for identifying such biases/microaggressions would be a start in the right direction. After training occurs, resources must be provided on what to do when one thinks he or she has been a victim or witnessed these behaviors as well. There should be an agency or department that is dedicated to investigating and remediating such issues.

Experiences with Training

Initially, when diversity training became available, I was relieved. I thought diversity training would cover racial diversity and microaggressions, as well as how to treat people from other cultures with sensitivity, tolerance, and respect. I became disappointed when I realized diversity training encompassed ideology that everyone is part of a "colorful fruit salad" and that diversity encompasses Baby Boomers, Generation Xers, and Generation Yers (Millennials). While this may be helpful in some cases, like in reducing ageism, it is not helpful in resolving conflicts between people of different races or cultures.

During training, we must identify that diversity is not just about working with persons of different ages but also of different cultures and racial backgrounds. Within diversity there is intersectionality, meaning one can belong to the same race and culture but identify or belong to a system of beliefs or religions largely synonymous with another culture.

Once employees go through training, there should be inclusion and sensitivity programs that occur throughout the year. These programs could include forums on race/racism with a third party acting as a moderator to lead the discussions. When I was hired as a teacher librarian for a large city, I spent an entire week in training. I was surprised to see that there was a forum on racism/racial biases in the school system and that there were independent workshops on similar topics that employees could attend.

We watched a video that contained a scene with an African American boy, an elderly Caucasian woman, and a Middle Eastern male shop owner. The video was in black and white. The video indicated someone was going to do something and we were supposed to anticipate what would happen. Right before the outcome occurred, the video was paused and we were asked to theorize on what would happen next with our peers. Quite a few people at my table said that the little African American boy was going to steal. My colleague (who happened to be African American as well) and I chimed in that the African American boy stealing was too obvious and a common misconception. We suspected that it was the elderly Caucasian woman because no one expected her to steal. Another person said that it was the shop owner who stole his own product to set up the boy.

When the video began to play again, we quickly saw the elderly white woman steal the candy, but the African American boy got blamed for it. My colleague and I felt so vindicated—but also angry—that the natural assumption was that the black boy was the thief. Our peers got quiet, and with that, we were moderated into another discussion about misconceptions that occurred while watching the film. We talked about our biases, we made real-world connections, and we told our stories willingly. I learned. They learned. In the end, my colleagues began to interact with me more. One woman confessed that without this particular session, she would have never taken the time to get to know me and my experiences.

Furthermore, she realized she hadn't thought about how her biases could affect the way she taught children of color or how she interacted with her minority colleagues. Overall, when we allow room for discussion that is moderated, intimate, and open, we allow room for inclusiveness. We allow room for change and room for opportunities that prepare us for how to deal with those from different backgrounds than ours. Granted, this doesn't happen overnight, but with constant opportunities to participate in such sessions, it can be a positive indicator for increasing inclusiveness within the organization.

Opportunities and Advancement

Inclusivity doesn't just exist within training, and it should be included when there are opportunities for promotion. For one, the library profession must think about how it is preparing minorities for the field and for promotion. Without applicable and constant data about how many minorities are in the profession, what types of preparation they are receiving for promotion or growth, and how many are currently in management positions, we will never be able to understand how we can help minorities. Library systems should also be encouraged to track their own metrics on this data to outline challenges that are preventing minorities from being awarded promotion. A former public library manager one day told me "there simply aren't enough qualified minorities out there." This is a stereotype.

Many qualified librarians are being looked over because the profession isn't inclusive. Racism in the library field isn't widely acknowledged. How can we correct or challenge a sentiment if it isn't acknowledged? We must research, we must reach out to those affected, and we must develop empathy. We must advocate. For centuries librarians have been the gatekeepers, protectors, and advocates for information. I believe it is at the root of what we do. We can advocate by speaking up and collecting data. We as librarians do not have to be "rabble rousers," but it is our obligation to make those in our organizations aware of the information that prohibits our internal patrons/workers from achieving their maximum potential.

By researching our organizations' current practices and policies, identifying outlying barriers or lack of inclusiveness, and surveying our peers on how to increase inclusivity (taking into account, race, culture, religion, and age), we as information professionals can start to develop a blueprint for transforming what inclusion should look like. In all, understanding as information professionals that we need to set our own personal biases aside, participate in training, participate in programs, participate in discussions, and participate in surveys that help us understand how our intercultural differences will allow us to move in a more positive direction. Furthermore, minority librarians must continue to "dismiss racism and stereotypes and rise beyond expectations; there should not be simply any distractions from our progress. As a result of innovation and constant change in library trends, we must take advantage of continuing educational programs. Being current with best practices supports opportunities to grow and also allows us to become competitive among other librarians" (Jackson, Jefferson & Nosakhere, 2012, 232). And most importantly, we must not give up hope as we press for more equality, more inclusions, and cultural sensitivity within the profession.

Historically Black Colleges and Universities

Lastly, I would like to mention that special institutions, such as Historically Black Colleges and Universities (HBCUs), should develop or continue training seminars on racial, ethnic, and cultural inclusion and sensitivity to bring awareness to cultural biases that exist within the workplace. HBCUs have a very profound history that is deeply connected to the African American church and other racially uplifting organizations, with most being founded in the years following emancipation from slavery and the end of the Civil War. Out of necessity, they offer a unique pedagogy centered on the history, self-perception, and self-growth of African American individuals and communities. This influence also affects the ways HBCUs conduct themselves, as they prepare both their traditional (African American) and nontraditional students from various nationalities and backgrounds for the challenges, as well as the opportunities, they face in society at large, and in the workforce occupations that exist beyond the campus setting.

In my experience, many persons from other cultures who are employed by such universities lack (or choose not to demonstrate) understanding regarding the emphasis on promoting the social and emotional as well as educational growth of young African Americans, who remain the majority of the student population in most HBCUs. Some of the comments that I have heard range from making crude remarks about the type of food served at such institutions to accusing other colleagues of being racist for expressing interests and desires to specifically help minority students. Often this reflects feelings and attitudes that the majority (white/Eurocentric) culture is not adequately reflected or dominant in the educational environment and population of these institutions. One needs to understand that in any academic environment, the needs of the target population may be greater than those of other populations. This does not mean that the needs of any of the enrolled populations will be ignored, but simply that the mission of the school is to prepare the target population to compete academically and professionally in a society that historically and statistically pays them less in income and charges more for basic needs and services (i.e., housing, health care, insurance, etc.).

There also needs to be support for other cultural/ethnic populations that are steadily increasing at these institutions. Librarians in particular must understand those cultural needs and provide seamless support for those students, encouraging their integration within Historically Black Colleges and Universities while helping them to celebrate and preserve their own cultural identities and traditions. This can be done by stepping out of our traditional silos and comfort zones and assuming new roles. Examples of this may include becoming advisors to student clubs and organizations that are not associated with our own cultural/ethnic backgrounds, showing genuine interest and a willingness to gain better understanding, and creating open and safe areas to promote dialogue amongst a variety of cultures. When we gain more understanding of others' beliefs, customs, and perceptions of the outside world (seeing things from multiple perspectives), we gain more understanding about our own beliefs, customs, and perceptions, and reduce our learned and subconscious biases through positive cultural exchanges and interactions.

Reference

Jackson, A. P. In Jefferson, J., & Nosakhere, A. (2012). *The 21st-century black librarian in America: Issues and challenges*. Lanham: Scarecrow Press.

Indigenous Support Staff in the Library

Maggie Mason Smith, *library specialist, Clemson University*

There is no universal definition of indigenous or tribal peoples. This chapter uses the term "Indigenous" as defined by the International Labour Organization (n.d.), which is "descent from populations, who inhabited the country or geographic region at the time of conquest, colonization or establishment of present state boundaries," and as a term describing Native American/Alaskan Natives, as well as any other tribal peoples to which these suggestions may be applied by a library organization working to build an inclusive and sensitive workplace culture.

When employees feel recognized, included, and respected, they are more productive and engaged in the workplace. In the field of librarianship, support staff may rarely experience these emotions on the job, and as the field has long struggled to recruit and retain a diverse employee population, this may be especially true of Indigenous library staff members. According to the demographics of the National Congress of American Indians (n.d.), pulled from results of the 2010 census, 2.9 million, or about 0.9 percent of the United States population identifies as American Indian/Alaskan Native; these numbers increase when considering members of the population that identify as American Indian/Alaskan Native as well as another race, changing to 5.2 million, or 1.7 percent of the US population. The American Library Association's (ALA) Diversity Counts Report (2009–10) indicates that the number of Native American/Alaskan Native Library Assistants (see tables A-2, and A-6 through A-8 as well as B2, and B-6 through B-8 of the report) increased from

1,258 to 1,700 between the years 2000 and 2009-10, for an increase of 442 staff members over the course of a decade. Inclusive recruitment and retention practices, sensitive workplace meetings and outings, and maintaining a visible Indigenous presence in the library will help to maintain or increase Indigenous representation within the profession.

Recruitment

Most administrators will agree that diversity among library staff is imperative. According to the ALA (2017), "In the library workforce, programs of recruitment, training, development, advancement and promotion are needed in order to increase and retain diverse library personnel who are reflective of the society" served (p. 1–2). Libraries generally wrestle with this task, but the ALA offers many helpful starting strategies on their Recruiting for Diversity webpage. Libraries should begin by establishing a diversity committee, charged with learning about the culture within the community and drafting a statement that outlines the library's values and goals, reflects a commitment to the overall experience of diverse support staff within the organization, and is publicly available. Based on the work of the committee, libraries can begin crafting thoughtful job postings, each with a description free of "any unnecessary qualifications that might prohibit the widest possible pool of applicants" (ALA, 2011). At this point, hiring committees reflective of the current state of diversity in the library can be created and given a clear "understanding of the position description, the preferred and minimum qualifications, and the selection criteria by which candidates will be evaluated," and instructed to "consider the potential benefits diverse or non-traditional applicants could provide to the positions, the institution, and the community served by the institution" whenever possible (ALA, 2011). These are positive steps toward sensitivity and inclusion in the workplace; with metrics in place, libraries can measure success and move forward with future recruitment needs.

Retention

Once a new employee is hired, focus should switch to retention, with emphasis on HR services and the cultural climate within the organization. The library's HR department should take advantage of the onboarding process to offer a comprehensive list of Indigenous-friendly, local resources, such as physical and mental health providers and ethnic grocers. HR should also develop and foster a mentorship program for newly hired support staff that will strengthen professional ties, build trust and support, and ultimately increase diversity in leadership roles. Library managers can participate in retention and support the cultural climate of the library by nurturing internal knowledge and talent through encouraging professional development. This may take the form of staff membership to the ALA's affiliate group, the American Indian Library Association (AILA); participation in conferences such as AILA's Joint Conference for Librarians of Color; or service on AILA's multiple committees. Managers may also encourage staff to create posters or host internal sessions demonstrating their professional development and use an intranet board to acknowledge the service that support staff are providing to the field of librarianship at large. Listservs and multicultural newsletters can be useful tools to help build community within the organization as well, and they can be used as an outlet to share public events or plan gatherings. The cultural climate of the library has a major impact on employee retention; having an HR and managerial plan in place is the best way to ensure that Indigenous staff have a positive first and ongoing experience in the workplace.

Policymaking

Library personnel policies should bolster the recruitment and retention of diverse support staff by ensuring that all employees are treated fairly. However, the needs of Indigenous staff are often overlooked at the time of policy creation. To mitigate this, library administration should consider both general and Indigenous-specific staff needs. First, as diversity is not always visible, an anonymous feedback form should be available to staff at all times. Next, to help employees recognize, understand, and accept cultural differences within the workplace, cultural competency trainings should be offered regularly, and employees should be encouraged to attend. When developing policy, libraries should pay particular attention to language; for example, the preferred local name of Indigenous tribes should always be used, and Indigenous People's Day could replace Columbus Day on all library signs and sites. Libraries may point to the precedent for this currently in place: Alaska, Hawaii, Oregon, South Dakota, and Vermont currently observe Indigenous People's Day. Flexible scheduling options should be offered for Indigenous staff that participate in tribal celebrations and benefits directly related to awareness and support for statistically higher health and mental health issues in the Indigenous community should be available, as well. Finally, sustainability, a major aspect of many Indigenous communities, should be a priority in the workplace. Personnel policies that ensure the fair treatment of all library support staff members, including those that are Indigenous, are key to creating an inclusive and sensitive workplace.

Workplace Gatherings

During the day-to-day management of the library, workplace meetings are essential as they aid in decision-making and provide an opportunity to exchange ideas and discuss objectives. All workplace meetings could begin with a statement of acknowledgement, recognizing the tribal land on which the library was built. There is no one correct way to acknowledge the traditional inhabitants of land, but the US Department of Arts and Culture (2017), describes acknowledgement as "a simple, powerful way of showing respect and a step toward correcting the stories and practices that erase Indigenous people's history and culture and toward inviting and honoring the truth." Workplace outings are also essential in that they renew creativity and provide a platform for casual social interaction while strengthening team cohesion. Ideas for diverse workplace outings include a trip to the nearest tribal library, visiting a nearby museum hosting a collection of tribal art, or having lunch at an ethnic restaurant. Potential "outings" that take place within the library include a diversity-centered book club, brown-bag lunch events where interested staff can discuss cultural values and share information about their heritage or hobbies, and diverse film showings. When planning meetings and outings, it is imperative that employers seek feedback (again, offering an anonymous option), give ample advance notice, and schedule events at a variety of times to ensure that all staff have the opportunity to participate if desired. Workplace gatherings that are sensitive to diversity will not only increase engagement and teamwork, they will also reinforce the desired culture of inclusion within the library.

Indigenous Presence

Whether or not employee gatherings are the setting for collection development decisions, event planning, or service design, it is important that support staff see themselves reflected in the collections, programs, and services they work so hard to offer. For Indigenous staff, this means that library holdings should include relevant works on all aspects of Indigenous culture and must contain works written by Indigenous authors, as well. But simply having relevant content is not enough—libraries should consider how Indigenous-centered works are defined and organized: are they shelved with folklore, myths, or legends rather than history, religion, or medicine (Justice, 2018)? If so, libraries may want to consider genrefication or a permanent, separate display of these works. Indigenous staff should also see themselves reflected in library programming and services. Libraries can reach out to the local Indigenous population to co-host or provide space for art exhibits, history lectures, language learning, land preservation workshops, and more, and using asset mapping, libraries can create and provide specific services to Indigenous peoples. Potential roadblocks to updated collections and inclusive programming and services are the same as those that may arise with any other diversity initiative and should be handled similarly. The ALA's Strategic Directions documentation provides a framework for library policy and decision-making and is useful in the event an explanation of library choices is required. Collections, programming, and services combine to create an atmosphere within the library; Indigenous library staff should be considered when working to make it an inclusive one.

Conclusion

It is easy to believe that recruitment and retention of diverse library support staff is predicated on inclusive and sensitive policy, procedure, and the overall climate within the library. Although it may seem that inclusive policy, procedure, and a sensitive workplace climate can only come from diversity-centered recruitment and retention. In reality, work to build an inclusive and sensitive workplace happens at all levels and in all aspects of library life. All employees are capable of exhibiting leadership and guidance that will inspire their peers to begin recognizing, appreciating, and including each other daily. Staff who feel seen, heard, and respected are far more likely to be productive and engaged—and perhaps most importantly they are more likely to be happy—in their jobs. So, it is imperative that Indigenous staff are not overlooked in the conversations around diversity, but are instead celebrated for the unique perspectives they can bring to the field. Only in this way will Indigenous representation increase within the library profession. The points and suggestions within this chapter regarding ways to encourage support staff through recruitment, retention, and day-to-day library functionality may serve as a foundation for libraries and library employees looking to demonstrate a commitment to Indigenous support staff in the workplace, through both their words and their actions.

Acknowledgment

The author would like to recognize the support of her husband, Nathan Smith, and mother-in-law, Lisa York Thompson, both of whom identify as Cherokee.

References

American Indian Library Association. (2018). Retrieved from https://ailanet.org/

American Library Association. (2009–10). Diversity counts report. Retrieved from http://www.ala.org/aboutala/sites/ala.org.aboutala/files/content/diversity/diversitycounts/diversitycountstables2012.pdf

American Library Association. (2011). Recruiting for diversity. Retrieved from http://www.ala.org/advocacy/diversity/workforcedevelopment/recruitmentfordiversity

American Library Association. (2017). Strategic directions. Retrieved from http://www.ala.org/aboutala/sites/ala.org.aboutala/files/content/governance/StrategicPlan/Strategic%20Directions%202017_Update.pdf

International Labour Organization. (n.d.). Who are the indigenous and tribal peoples? Retrieved from https://www.ilo.org/global/topics/indigenous-tribal/WCMS_503321/lang--en/index.htm

Justice, D.H. (Producer). (2018). Indigenous literature, social justice, and the decolonial library [Video webinar]. Retrieved from http://www.choice360.org/librarianship/webinars/indigenous-literatures

National Congress of American Indians. (n.d.). Demographics. Retrieved from http://www.ncai.org/about-tribes/demographics

United States Department of Arts and Culture. (2017). Honor native land: A guide and call to acknowledgement. Retrieved from https://usdac.us/nativeland/

14

Organizational Change and Gender Identity
When Good Intentions Fall Short

Alex Byrne, *youth services librarian, Pierce County Library System*

I have an official work badge with my pronouns on it. They're readable, they're present, and it's rather nice to have them. I can count on my fingers, however, how many people there are at my worksite that consistently use those pronouns to refer to me. I've never been part of a cohort in my organization where there's been more than three people who have the same gender presentation that I do. It took a lot of hollering, both inside and outside the organization, to make things like pronouns on badges happen, but they are here. I fear that my organization hasn't taken the right lesson out of this. I would have liked to have seen more practical steps taken to be more open and welcoming for everyone, such as training staff on how to ask for pronouns, strategizing ways to bring more gender presentations to staff cohorts, or engaging workshops and training to help staff understand the many ways gender can be presented, and revising name policies to take the name that a person says is their name, rather than what is on their driver's license or other form of identification. These are some of the proactive steps the organization could take, instead of waiting for and then reacting to a loud and sustained voice telling them to do something. Even so, work badges with pronouns on them is an improvement from how things were.

Committee Charge and Discharge

I had the opportunity in 2017 to participate on a system-wide committee, composed solely of non-supervisors, focusing on fostering a better workplace culture. This committee came about because in previous years, an outside organization had surveyed the library system's workers to get our responses on what we thought was working well and what wasn't, and there had been a consistently lower score in the realm of the culture, and it hadn't improved in the years between the surveys. So our committee came to be, looking for the elusive element that would make things better.

Most of us didn't have much experience with how to solicit the opinions of our co-workers, but we did our best, in conversation and in survey, and we got a fair number of responses to our questions about how frontline staff felt about their supervisors, about higher management, and about what we could do to make our organization a better place. We packaged them up into a presentation and a report, and we gave that report to a wide swath of the upper-management team with our recommendations on how to make things better. It felt like progress to be able to have the attention of the people who could do something about the situation, giving them a report that they had asked for. This was the place for the rousing speech that changed everything for the better, at least in the stories we had created in our heads.

Reality, unfortunately, is not nearly that kind, and it reminded us of that fact as soon as the response came through. We were thanked for our work and told that they were already implementing most of our recommendations. We wanted higher-level management to come out to the branches more *and* do some frontline work to understand the environment of working in a branch and the situations that came up. They said they were already visiting branches and learning from them while they were there.

We were looking for training of staff on the issues that were broadly reflected across society: equity, diversity, inclusion, and proper use of names and pronouns. And we got some training on those subjects, although there was still room for improvement. However, I am still waiting for the rest of our group's recommendations to be implemented. And I am still waiting for a consistent number of people to use the pronouns displayed on my badge correctly and consistently. I know I'm not alone in being frustrated that management doesn't always embrace the change that staff finds necessary, even when they've asked for input.

Trust and Change

Managers and supervisors are a crucial part of organizational change. To increase equity, diversity, and inclusion in their staff and their public services, managers and supervisors must first show that they are ready to make decisions that will support it. If this is not the case, no amount of suggestions, solicitations, or outside consultants can help the organization. Employees advocating for issues like gender identity will want to see management consistently and publicly demonstrate that they are trustworthy and publicly committed to equity, diversity, and inclusion.

Without trust in managers and supervisors, ideas disappear long before they can be articulated. Much of that trust comes from managers being willing to lead by example. If a supervisor has their pronouns on their name badge, I can be reasonably assured they understand why that is important, and we can talk about more advanced things regarding gender identity and presentation, rather than having to assume that if I want to talk about these things, I will first have to educate the supervisor about the importance of pronouns before we can go further. It should not be the burden of employees to educate their supervisors.

One of the recommendations from the 2017 survey that hasn't been fully implemented was for our upper management to provide a direct feedback mechanism, where people could submit ideas and concerns they were having on topics that could affect the organization as a whole, and where management, or appropriate committees, would guarantee a response to them within a certain time frame. This would boost confidence in any library's management in several ways:

- Knowing where to put an idea makes it easier to make suggestions.
- Knowing there will be some sort of guaranteed response will increase participation, because no library worker wants to feel like they've wasted their time shouting into a void.
- Making decisions in public and providing as much public information about those decisions as possible increases a library staff's confidence in knowing what their supervisors and managers will think about a particular suggestion. If a supervisor or manager is known for taking a suggestion or an idea, examining it seriously and critically, and then making an informed and public decision about that idea, it makes staff submissions of suggestions more likely.

Grassroots Change

I've come to the realization that to spark success in my library—an organization that prizes change and learning as one of its core skills and qualities—I must not let my own spark die. I need to take personal responsibility for change. Waiting for it to come from above is not enough. For example, I can

- attend workshops and programs about the things that i am waiting for, using the money set aside for travel, and conferences, and learning opportunities;
- bring those ideas back and seed them among the people in my cohorts and locations and explain why these things are important;
- push back and provide suggestions to my supervisor and those managers whose ears i can bend, to accomplish something informally when there is no place to try and accomplish something formally;
- give my approval to good ideas, encourage them when they add to what has been missing, and strive for each of them to contain a more complete picture than what may have been intended, but what is instead surely and sorely needed;
- make my policy rulings about inclusion consistent and welcoming to those who need it, to protect them from those who think they do not deserve it; and, perhaps most importantly,
- recognize when good work has been done, celebrate it, and encourage it, so that more might happen.

If I can do these things, I can create the environment that I want to work in, and by extension, help others do the same. That's the kind of change I want to see.

15

Virginia Commonwealth University Libraries' Gender-Inclusive Work Group Experience

M. Teresa Doherty, *assistant head for information services, Virginia Commonwealth University*
Donna E. Coghill, *community engagement librarian, Virginia Commonwealth University*

As with many large libraries, Virginia Commonwealth University (VCU) Libraries staff includes individuals who identify as transgender or gender-nonconforming/nonbinary. The March 7, 2018 charge from VCU Libraries Management Council, a group representing division and department heads across our libraries, to the Gender-Inclusive Work Group was to "identify ways that systems, services and spaces can be more welcoming to transgender or gender-nonconforming/nonbinary library users, and supporting users in the case of non-legal name changes." This work reflects the mission of the university and the library in terms of diversity, equity, and inclusion, and we soon realized that changes we make to benefit our students will also benefit our faculty and staff, in a "rising tide lifts all boats" approach. We will use the group report to discuss how VCU Libraries can improve our work environment in order to retain our current transgender and nonbinary staff as well as attract new staff to join us in the future.

The gender-inclusive work group for VCU Libraries includes Erin White, head of digital engagement and work group chair; Stephen Barkley, operations librarian; Donna E. Coghill, community engagement librarian; Teresa Doherty, assistant head for information services; and Liam Palmer, collections analyst. The group Administrative Council liaison is Jimmy Ghaphery, the AUL for scholarly communications and publishing.

Information Gathering

Early on, we reached out to our library student worker community, asking for students who identify as transgender or gender-nonconforming/nonbinary to work with us. Managers of student employees were sent an invitation that they would send to *all* student employees rather than singling students out, and four student workers joined us for one targeted meeting. With support from library administration, students who participated were able to count the time spent with the committee as hours worked and their recommendations as both patrons and employees formed a core portion of our recommendations. We also met with our library's undergraduate advisory committee, seeking additional input from our students.

The student workers provided much needed input from their lived experiences that could not have been gained in any other way. They suggested several areas that needed work: additional gender-neutral restrooms, signage to aid in finding restrooms, and a greater availability of sanitation bins and sanitary products. When a suggestion was made to add signage in our current large restrooms alerting users that single stall gender-neutral restrooms were available elsewhere in our building, they responded that "people who do not use these restrooms—for whatever reason—will never see that message." With that additional context, our recommendation is to place such signage in other locations, including next to the doors to these restrooms, on the outside. Sanitation bins are easily accessible in restrooms designated for women, but they are not available in spaces designated for men. We recommended that such disposal bins be purchased and installed in all of our restrooms.

Gender-neutral restrooms are particularly necessary in the medical library. One student worker noted "I wouldn't drink the whole day (at work)" in order to avoid the gendered restrooms. He continued "the only single stall restroom is in the employee area." Avoiding outing himself at work, this restroom would also be avoided.

These library student workers who identify as transgender or gender-non-conforming/nonbinary also focused on the concern of being outed at work due, in part, to their name of use, and discussed the issues students face with name changes on campus. Said one student "you feel like you have to out yourself to each new group of people you meet, in a new job." They also commented that "A lot of time people don't have practice using different pronouns and I don't always like to be the person being practiced upon. Just practice by yourself, it's not difficult." One suggestion they felt strongly about was our adding an option of pronouns for name tags as well as staff training on best practices for pronouns in a customer service setting. These suggestions were integral to the group work and the final report.

As all library committees know, the first task is to conduct a literature review, and we quickly located a number of articles that informed our recommendations, some of which were shared in our final report, including (but not limited to) the following resources:

- Inclusive Restroom Design (Schwartz, M. [2018]. Inclusive restroom design. *Library Journal*, 143[8], 28–31)
- Libraries as Safe Spaces for LGBT+ Patrons (Aycock, A. [2018]. Libraries as safe spaces for LGBT+ patrons. *Information Today*, 35[3], 6–7)
- Transgender Inclusion Institutional Assessment Worksheet (Garber-Pearson, R., Kim, S., Kehrein, M., & Yogi, B. Transgender Inclusion Institutional Assessment Worksheet, Google Doc, November 2017, https://docs.google.com/document/d/1rzosIL7gKyXTbvN_eZa-x5H pRIbuL1rGZCrAhsETu88/edit)

We also conducted an environmental scan, by reaching out to a variety of library discussion groups, as well as to specific libraries in our state and those which we consider our peers, asking for "best practices for gender inclusion," and examples of how they are creating welcoming spaces, systems, and services. We also looked at university-level support for trans and gender non-conforming communities at VCU to get a sense of the environment on campus, and we asked library employees via an anonymous survey what information they needed to better understand these issues.

Actions and Plans

Our first short-term goal—to implement each student's name of use in our ILS—was accomplished in less than two months. Students are able to submit name-of-use change requests to various university units, such as recreational sports and the library.

After discovering the most efficient process for updating our students' names of use in our library systems, we realized that we could offer library staff the same option. We have approximately 125 full-time library staff across our four libraries, including our location in Doha, Qatar. Of that number, almost 30 percent use a variation of their legal name as their work name, including those who use their middle name, a nickname, or initials. In our workgroup, three of the five staffers use a different name, so we piloted a staff name of use in patron records and staff ILS profiles with these staffers. We intend to reach out and offer this to all library staff colleagues.

We also dove deep into the libraries' current practices, discovering that we had already implemented a number of procedures and services that other libraries were still debating.

For example, in Cabell Library, we have three single-stall, all-gender restrooms, two of which have been available since 2010, and a third which was intentionally built as part of a recent renovation and construction project completed in March 2016. Our sister library on the medical campus, which is in a much smaller and older building, does have a single-stall, all-gender restroom for staff use; however, its presence and location are not well known, even by staff in that building, since it has no signage, and is located off the staff kitchen. It is not currently available to patrons.

In addition, any library staff have participated in Safe Zone training, a two-hour workshop offered by VCU University Counseling Services that sets the basis for being an LGBTQIA ally by helping to reduce homophobia, transphobia, biphobia, and heterosexism. One of our librarians (and member of the Gender-Inclusive work group), Donna E. Coghill, co-authored and facilitates Trans Sensitivity in Policing, a workshop on strategies for serving trans and gender-nonconforming people, which has been taught at every VCU Police Academy since 2015.

Further examples of things we had already implemented include the following:

- VCU Libraries job announcements were reviewed and updated to remove gendered pronouns.
- Some library staff have opted to include their personal gender pronouns in email signatures, on business cards, and when introducing themselves.
- In June 2011, we initiated a service to provide library borrowing privileges to faculty spouses and partners, so that they can borrow materials from our collections on their own separate and confidential patron account. VCU Libraries was an on-campus leader in partner benefits, and even renamed this program "Faculty Partner Borrowing," based on discoveries during our group work.

Library administrative review of our work group's recommendations resulted in suggestions for actions which our library could implement immediately, and for actions which would require additional investment of time, energy, or funding. Recommendations for immediate action include

- adding pronouns and safe zone logos to staff web profiles, when requested;
- installing feminine hygiene disposal receptacles in all restroom stalls, gendered and universal restrooms;
- creating a webpage for the university community on our gender-inclusive efforts;
- increasing awareness of gender-neutral restrooms; and
- creating training opportunities for library staff on gender-inclusive pronouns and language.

The following recommendations would require greater investment of time and money. They would greatly benefit staff and patrons by offering additional and important layers of visible equality. These include

- updating signage to make our gender-neutral restrooms easier to locate;
- encouraging more staff to participate in campus led safe zone training;
- registering for and promoting orcid as a non-gendered scholarly identification system;
- updating/converting additional all-gender restroom facilities; and
- hiring a diversity and inclusion librarian.

The changes below have already been implemented and help create the most welcoming environment for our staff:

- Our printed floor maps have been updated to show the locations of all-gender restrooms.
- One library vending machine now stocks feminine hygiene products.
- Our business office has updated the business card template to include personal pronouns.
- Our ILS now uses our institutional eID or other unique identifiers instead of names in our automated email notifications.
- Staff who have requested the use of their preferred name in our ILS will see that name in their account profile as well as in their own patron records.

Our work is far from complete as library administration continues to review the report and makes decisions on implementation. Nevertheless, we are confident that the work of this group will benefit our library staff as well as our students—perhaps even more so.

Creating an Effective Student Employment Environment

Stephanie Van Ness, *Northern Arizona University*

Supervising student employees in an academic library offers various challenges. Although there is more research, engagement, and discussion than years past on the topic, managing student employees still tends to be the responsibility of an entry-level supervisory position, and anecdotally speaking, the level of support for these roles varies wildly by institution. Academic libraries are in an era of rapid and frequent change, and this time presents a wonderful opportunity to provide an equitable and beneficial work environment for library student employees.

In over ten years supervising student employees in an academic library, I've seen a dramatic shift not only in my own approach to supervising students, but also in the level of work and ability I see in my team. Given the right environment, traditional students can be thoughtful, engaged contributors to your library's mission, values, and goals. After all, in addition to being employees, they're an academic library's target audience—and they're gold mines of ideas and information. However, student employees and their managers may encounter the kinds of biases that persist about college students in general, and these perceptions hinder the efficiency and effectiveness of not just employees, but the entire unit or library. Just because student employees may often be young and inexperienced, that doesn't mean that they are any less entitled to a respectful, equitable, and engaging work experience where they can grow, balance their work and life, and contribute meaningfully to the organization. While it's easy to link treating employees this way to higher productivity and efficiency, it's also just the ethical way to treat human beings who work for us.

When I began my career in academic libraries in 2008, my role included co-supervising upwards of 25 student employees. Truthfully, when I began supervising students I had very little experience; our hiring practices were minimal, and the job description wasn't clear and was even intentionally vague in some ways (which I now know was a terrible idea). Our interviews, likewise, were too vague for us to accurately determine a candidate's fit for the organizational culture we wanted to build. Not surprisingly, turnover in my unit was higher than it needed to be and I spent a lot of time managing performance issues. Many students did the bare minimum, a few rose above the norm if they already had a strong work ethic (but quickly grew tired of picking up others' slack), and some were just here for a paycheck, cutting corners wherever they could.

Improving the Foundation

In retrospect, the single most important change I made in the student employment environment I oversee was to change my hiring practices. I set about learning everything I could about hiring employees. I consistently review interview questions and focus heavily on soft skills rather than experience specific to the library environment, I tweak the job description anytime it needs it, and I changed the title of the position to something more intentional and linked to what I was looking for (Main Desk Aide seems to say, "sit at the Main Desk," whereas "User Experience Assistant" says "provide a positive user experience in a variety of ways!"). In an attempt to recruit a diverse pool of applicants, I send the recruitment message to key offices and groups on campus rather than waiting for whomever stumbles past the job on the university's hiring site.

It can be time-consuming to hire student employees with an approach similar to one we might use for full-time employees (there's a happy medium between putting in some extra effort to hire well and doing a full-on several-month search), but it's worth it. Hiring this way means being intentional down to the word about the job description and job advertisement, saying clearly what the job is and isn't, and having a high standard for applications that include cover letters and resumes. Additionally, the interview process includes questions that are at a professional level. The students work hard to get in here, but the payoff is that they have an engaging work environment where they can develop professionally. Furthermore, I'm best able to provide that environment by preemptively reducing the amount of time I spend addressing performance issues and hiring new employees.

Secondly, intentional training is imperative, and I enjoy the privilege of a thorough, engaging training program run by one of my colleagues. By using Blackboard Learn, we're able to provide a blended-format training that immerses our students in the library environment, assesses their retention of what they learn, and provides structure to our blended learning approach to student employee learning. The robust training we provide now is a tremendous improvement on the learn-by-shadowing method I inherited, and even the classroom approach I later developed (so many hours of me talking!). While not every library is fortunate to have a staff member whose primary role is devoted to training, the value of such a role cannot be overstated and has been key to the productivity and engagement I see from my unit's student employees now.

Work That Matters

Employees at all levels of the organization need work that they care about and see the value of doing, and student employees are no exception. If we give students work for the sake of work, with some misguided notion that they must be doing something at all times, they see right through it. With clear values and job duties that link back to those values, students will demonstrate very early and clearly whether they're the right fit for the job, and most will go well above and beyond because they feel like they are valued in their organization. For our part, students have helped tremendously to provide services in a time when we not only implement major change (our library implemented both a new LMS and a new website last year, to name but two examples), but also increasingly heavy staff workloads as we expand services to meet the needs of our ever-growing university population. In one example, when we needed to test a product to determine whether it would work to allow customers to self-book our multimedia equipment, a student employee set up most of the information we needed within the software and tested how it would function at our service point, then competently presented her findings to staff. Another example focused on the intranet policies and procedures pages for our unit's service desk, which needed a major overhaul. Because my own workload wasn't going to allow me time to write the necessary updates, I delegated the work to a team of three student employees, who did a beautiful job learning the software needed, updating and editing documents, and building a new page from scratch. In both of these examples, student employee input, knowledge, and engagement proved invaluable to our unit and our library.

Employees cannot work at the level described in those two examples without a strong foundation of context, training, and creative latitude to thrive. By providing student employees with structured, thorough, and assessed training, they have a strong sense of where they fit into our organization and into the university community. They not only learn the basic skills of the job, but they also learn service values, introduce themselves to staff around the library to learn our organizational structure and what roles other people perform here, and how it all connects. It's easy to dismiss this key component of a workplace for any part-time, temporary employee, but it makes a world of difference in how they perceive their role and effectiveness on a job. Furthermore, our student employees receive thorough, intentional performance evaluations based on the National Association of Colleges and Employers career readiness competencies identified for college students' successful entry into the professional workforce. Students also use the same form to write self-evaluations, which provide them the opportunity to self-reflect and see how the work they do here relates to what they might do in future careers.

Creating enriching, engaging student employment environments goes beyond the work itself. For example, I teach student employees that the customer is *not* always right (sometimes customers are just mean), they have clear latitude to leave any customer interaction that makes them feel uncomfortable, we don't need a doctor's note for every call-in sick, and we don't need unnecessary "rules for the sake of rules." For every policy, there should be a concrete and important "why" behind it. Student employees have human problems just like full-time employees, but often without the benefit of sick time or the other allowances that enable us to balance our lives. Furthermore, when we foster an employment culture in which ALL employees are treated equitably and with respect, these students graduate knowing what a functional and respectful work environment looks like, hopefully making them more likely to stand up and advocate against poor working conditions elsewhere.

Taking all of these actions isn't enough if we don't assess our progress, including asking for employees' genuine, unfiltered input. For me, that input partly comes in the form of an anonymous survey in which the students I supervise can evaluate my performance as a supervisor, their job functions, and their work environment. I do not share these survey results widely, and I do not seek IRB approval to do so because I want to avoid tarnishing the intent of the survey: to listen to my employees and act on their concerns when possible. I do, however, share the full, unfiltered results with my supervisor, in the interest of transparency and accountability. I also encourage asking questions anytime some aspect of their responsibilities seems unpleasant or inefficient; the answer is never "just do it," but rather "here's why we do it this way. What isn't working?" Sometimes the only answer I can provide is more context, and occasionally I give guidance regarding expectations and not always liking every aspect of our jobs. However, dismissing student employee concerns just because they come from people who are perceived as "young," "entitled," or any of the other stereotypes we see attributed to college students would only create an atmosphere of discontent for the employees—and more work for the supervisor, who inevitably must deal with the effects of that discontent.

Getting Other Leaders On Board

Even when you work hard to create an atmosphere of trust, engagement, and respect for student employees, there is always that next level. Those who manage students (other than in the smallest libraries) are not often also in the position to make major decisions that can have the biggest impact on student employees. Everything above takes time and iteration, as well as tenacity in the face of setbacks.

Speaking with leaders in your organization about the conditions that affect employee experience can involve some uncomfortable conversations and standing up even if it feels risky, especially for those who are low in the hierarchy themselves. Advocating for student employees can be even harder, since various stereotypes and age-related biases exist about college students in general; examples I've encountered include notions that students are less likely to work hard, or that young people somehow deserve to be paid less than they need to live.

However, it is important not to go into these conversations blindly. We can advocate for our employees most efficiently by knowing our organizations well (including big-picture aspects, like what kinds of pressures are coming from above, even at the government level), knowing our administrators well, and being able to appeal in a variety of contexts (for example, the person who manages your money wants to see you're spending efficiently, whereas the person who does your marketing and outreach more likely wants to see that your unit and your employees are representing your library well). While advocacy requires taking a stand when it's necessary, it also requires listening to the other side, taking in context, being open to new information, and compromising with diplomacy. If you're seen as the one who fights and is all take and no give, you are doing your employees and anyone else for whom you advocate a disservice.

Is All This Effort Worth It?

I currently manage student employees in an environment where I am not able to pay them competitively compared to off-campus employers. This chapter isn't the place to get into the local and institutional politics behind why, but my biggest takeaway is that overall, *they stay*, even though they can leave and make at least one to two dollars more per hour by working off campus. Turnover isn't cheap—it costs about $1,000 in staff time, student training time, etc. to hire a student in the role I supervise, plus the incalculable loss in institutional memory of the one who left—so the longer I can get them to stay, the better for us. It's also a benefit to the students; they leave college with a job where they stayed several years, and in many cases demonstrate professionally responsible experience. Most importantly: they've seen what it is to be respected and valued in their work, how to diplomatically question authority, and how to be creative in their work.

This kind of work is never done. Times change. Your organizations need change. Societal norms change. Being ready to adapt, advocate, and be inclusive is key to maintaining a positive work environment for everyone, regardless of their rank in a hierarchy.

Shared Understanding and Accountability through a Library Code of Conduct

Amanda H. McLellan, *assistant director for discovery and technology services,*
East Carolina University

Though documents of professional ethics have existed for many years, as our workplaces and professional meeting spaces have become more diverse, new needs arise. In recent years, many conferences and organizations have adopted codes of conduct to help lay a foundation of understanding acceptable behavior in the workplace. In 2017, the Joyner Library Diversity Committee discussed the trend and thought it might be an interesting exercise to draft a code of conduct for the library.

The goals of drafting a code of conduct were threefold: the Joyner Library Diversity Committee wanted to ensure the varied university resources that might be of assistance were compiled in one place, we wanted to reaffirm our commitment to making our workplace the best to our ability, and we wanted a public document so that potential employees could see that Joyner Library is committed to diversity and accountability. We wanted this to be a library-wide effort, with input from the various stakeholders. We also wanted a document that is flexible and could adjust to the future needs of the library.

One question that came up was enforcement of this document. Since the Joyner Library Diversity Committee is not a governing body, our intent was not to make a procedure for enforcement, duplicate what already exists, or bypass/override library and university procedure.

With those things in mind, the Joyner Library Diversity Committee looked at examples from other organizations and compiled a draft. This draft was sent to the Library Director, who gave us her blessing to move forward. This draft was made available to the entire library, and an open forum was set so that people could come and give feedback. It was very important to our committee that this be a grassroots document, with many opportunities for input. Those who could not attend were free to edit the draft in Google Docs or send email. Several library staff came and gave excellent feedback, asked questions that helped us clarify our language, and made suggestions to strengthen the document. The draft was then sent to the university's Office of Equity and Diversity for review, and they made minor suggestions, and ensured alignment with university policies and procedures.

The Director's Executive Council reviewed this and suggested to call this document a "Statement of Acceptable Behavior," as they wanted to avoid confusion. Some felt "code" implied an enforceable procedure. This is a fair critique, and if other institutions wish to adopt a similar document, this seems like a reasonable alternative title. Another suggestion was that we move recommended resources to a separate document that would be easier to edit. We have created this document, and it resides in the Library Diversity Committee's shared folder. I was able to present a poster on our statement at University of North Carolina Charlotte's Diversity Day, February 2019, where several people asked if there was resistance from staff. Since the Library Diversity Committee made every effort to gather feedback from staff, and the statement itself does not outline punishable action, response from library employees was positive.

Our statement is available online, under "About Us," and made available here in print.

Joyner Library Statement of Acceptable Conduct

INTRODUCTION
This document was created by the Diversity Committee, with input from additional employees of Joyner Library. We created it because we believe that articulating our values and obligations to one another reinforces the already high regard in which we hold our colleagues. Having such a statement also provides us with clear guidance for appropriate and professional behavior. The guide below aims to provide Joyner employees opportunities to enrich our discussions.

SCOPE
This document applies to our interactions in various areas of our shared professional lives, including those within Joyner Library, those that take place over email and social media when representing ECU and Joyner Library, and at conferences and other events where we represent ECU and Joyner Library.

VALUES

We want Joyner Library to be a fun, productive, and safe space for everyone. In addition to upholding our core values of respect and honesty, there are several ways we can accomplish this:

Our collaboration with departments and divisions within the library and university, as well as with community members and organizations, is key to our success. We view colleagues and patrons as our peers and collaborators. We maintain open lines of communication and foster good working relationships with our colleagues.

We believe in inclusion, not merely because it's a mechanism for happier, more productive teams, but also because we believe we have an obligation to work against structural discrimination. We work to fulfill this obligation in myriad ways— for example, by adhering fairly to University hiring and promotion policies, investing in community outreach efforts, and reinforcing an organizational culture which supports diversity. This Statement of Acceptable Conduct plays a critical role in those efforts.

EXPECTED BEHAVIORS

Every member of Joyner Library is expected to come to work ready to do their best, be considerate of their colleagues, and contribute to a collaborative, positive, and healthy environment in which we can all succeed.

Be supportive of your colleagues, both proactively and responsively. Offer to help if you see someone struggling or otherwise in need of assistance, taking care not to be patronizing or disrespectful. If someone approaches you looking for help, be generous with your time; if you're under a deadline, direct them to someone else who may be of assistance. Go out of your way to include people in division/department conversations and social activities in an effort to build an environment free of cliques. However, also respect coworkers' right to opt out of social activities unrelated to their jobs and recognize that their non-participation may not indicate disinterest in your mutual work.

Be collaborative. Be welcoming, friendly, patient, and inclusive. Involve your colleagues (including supervisees, when appropriate) in brainstorms, goal setting, planning documents, and the like. Recognize the value in both asking others for feedback and sharing yours with them.

Be considerate. Our work depends on the work of those around us. Any decision you make will affect patrons and colleagues, and you should take those consequences into account when making decisions. Assuming tone and intent through writing, such as email, is a commonplace for misunderstanding. Try to give your colleagues the benefit of the doubt when reading, and please take extra care when writing to try to avoid misunderstanding.

Be humane. Be polite and friendly in all forms of communication, especially online communication, where opportunities for misinterpretation are greater. Use sarcasm carefully. Tone is especially hard to decipher online. Be careful in the words that you choose. Remember that sexist, racist, and other exclusionary jokes can be offensive to those around you. Be kind to others. Do not insult or put down other people.

Be respectful. Not all of us will agree all the time, but disagreement is no excuse for poor behavior or poor manners. We might all experience some frustration now and then, but we cannot allow that frustration to turn into a personal attack or violence. It's important to remember that a workplace where people feel uncomfortable or threatened is not a productive one.

UNACCEPTABLE BEHAVIORS

ECU protected classes are: Disability, Sexual Orientation, Race/Ethnicity, Age, Sex, Gender Identity, Color, Veteran Status, Genetic Information, Political Affiliation, National Origin, and Religion. Discrimination and harassment are expressly prohibited in University Policy. Discrimination is defined as actions that subject individuals to unfavorable or unequal treatment based on a protected class. Harassment is unwelcome conduct based on a protected class. Sexual harassment is any unwelcome sexual comment, request for sexual favors, or other unwanted conduct of a sexual nature. Prohibited Conduct includes, but is not limited to, sexual assault, offensive touching, sexual exploitation, dating and domestic violence, sexual- or gender-based harassment, complicity, and retaliation. Joyner Library is committed to providing a welcoming and safe environment for all people.

This Statement of Acceptable Conduct also discourages any behavior or language which is unwelcoming. Some unwelcoming behavior takes the form of microaggressions—subtle put-downs which may be unconsciously delivered. Regardless of intent, microaggressions can have a significant negative impact on people and have no place on our team. (For a helpful article on microaggressions, see https://www.psychologytoday.com/us/blog/microaggressions-in-everyday-life/201011/microaggressions-more-just-race.)

REPORTING A PROBLEM

These guidelines are ambitious, and we're not always going to succeed in meeting them. When something goes wrong—whether it's a microaggression or an instance of harassment—there are a number of things you can do to address the situation with your colleagues. We know that you'll do your best work if you're happy and comfortable in your surroundings. Depending on your comfort level and the severity of the situation, here are some things you can do to address it:

Address it directly. If you're comfortable bringing up the incident with the person who initiated it, request that the person discuss with you how their behavior affected you. Be sure to approach these conversations in a forgiving spirit: an angry or tense conversation will not do either of you any good. If you're unsure how to go about that, try asking your supervisor or the Office of Equity and Diversity for advice on discussion points first—they have resources for how to make this conversation happen, especially within the Conflict Resolution and Mediation Program (https://conflict-resolution.ecu.edu/).

If you don't think having a direct conversation is a good option, there are a number of alternate routes you can take.

1. **Talk to a peer or mentor.** Your colleagues are likely to have personal and professional experience on which to draw that could be of use to you. If you have someone you're comfortable approaching, reach out and discuss the situation with them. They may be able to advise on how they would handle it or direct you to someone who can. The flip side of this, of course, is that you should also be available if your colleagues reach out to you.

2. **Talk to your supervisor or the Library Director.** Your supervisor probably knows quite a lot about the dynamics of your team, which makes them a good person to ask for advice. They may also be able to talk directly to the colleague in question if you feel uncomfortable or unsafe doing so yourself. Finally, your supervisor will try to help you figure out how to ensure that any conflict with a colleague doesn't interfere with your work.

3. **Talk to the Office of Equity and Diversity (OED).** If you feel that you have been harassed or discriminated against by a university employee, student, or visitor based on one of the university's protected classes outlined, or allege retaliation related to these complaints, you may fill out an online grievance reporting form (http://www.ecu.edu/cs-acad/oed/grievance-form.cfm) or you may contact the Office for Equity and Diversity at oed@ecu.edu or 252-328-6804.

TAKING CARE OF EACH OTHER

Sometimes, you may witness behavior that seems like it isn't aligned with our values. Err on the side of caring for your colleagues in situations like these. Even if an incident seems minor, reach out to the person affected to check in, or possibly ask another colleague you know they are close with to check in. In certain situations, it may also be helpful to speak directly to the person who has potentially misrepresented this Statement of Acceptable Conduct, a manager, or OED directly to voice your concerns.

COMMITTING TO IMPROVEMENT

We understand that none of us are perfect: It's expected that all of us, regardless of our backgrounds, will from time to time fail to live up to our very high standards. What matters is owning up to your mistakes and making a clear and persistent effort to improve. If someone lets you know that you have acted (consciously or otherwise) in a way that might make your colleagues feel unwelcome, refrain from being defensive; remember that if someone approaches you with a concern, it likely took a great deal of courage for them to do so. The best way to respect that courage is to acknowledge your possible mistake, apologize, and move on—with a renewed commitment to do better.

FURTHER READING

To address the many forms of harassment and discrimination, the University has policies and regulations in place including, but not limited to, the Notice of Non-discrimination and Affirmative Action Policy and the Regulation Sexual Harassment and Gender-Based Harassment and Other Forms of Interpersonal Violence. These policies and regulations are posted widely and are available on the OED's web-site at www.ecu.edu/oed and the University Policy Manual at www.ecu.edu/PRR. OED welcomes the opportunity to speak with anyone who has concerns, questions, or would like additional information about the Office's policies, programs, and resources. They also maintain a lending library and frequently offer further educational opportunities.

ADDITIONAL RESOURCES*

Author's note—this section was moved to a separate document in Joyner Library's statement, but I left it here to show you what sort of things we include.

Bromley, P., & Orchard, C. D. (2016). Managed morality: The rise of professional codes of conduct in the U.S. nonprofit sector. Nonprofit and Voluntary Sector Quarterly, 45(2), 351–374. https://doi.org/10.1177/0899764015584062

Oliver, P. (2018, July 18). Taking criticism while privileged. Retrieved from: https://www.insidehighered.com/advice/2018/07/18/advice-dealing -criticism-person-privilege-academe-opinion

Schomberg J., and Cole K. (2017, Apr 19). Hush...: The dangers of silence in academic libraries. Retrieved from: http://www.inthelibrarywiththeleadpipe .org/2017/hush-the-dangers-of-silence-in-academic-libraries/

LICENSE

CREDIT

Much of this document was adapted from the following resources:
- http://code-of-conduct.voxmedia.com/
- http://projectinclude.org/writing_cocs#write-and-communicate-a-clear -anti-harassment-policy
- http://web.archive.org/web/20141109123859/http://speakup.io/coc.html

---

Note that this is a living document, so it can and *should* change, and may have already changed from publication of this book. It is licensed Creative Commons (CC-BY), so feel free to adopt and adapt for your institution.

Building a Library Employee Appreciation Committee

Jennifer Natale, *liaison librarian, Appalachian State University*

L ibrary employees spend a large portion of their week at their place of employment, the Library! Our work hours are much more satisfying when we work well with those around us and we feel that our efforts have a positive effect on the organization. A Library Employee Appreciation Committee can serve as a positive force in the workplace to boost morale, connect individuals across the library, and to provide opportunities to appreciate outstanding contributions.

The Committee

The University Libraries Employee Appreciation Committee is charged with recognizing the outstanding contributions of library employees. The committee will implement activities that build community among library employees and will plan an annual event celebrating and recognizing outstanding service and achievements.

In October of 2016, a task force at Appalachian State University was charged with developing parameters for an Employee Appreciation Committee and processes for recognizing the accomplishments of personnel in University Libraries. A list of outcomes was developed and a timeline was established to complete the work. The task force collected ideas of employee appreciation programs and committees from other university libraries as well as other organizations. Task force members talked to all teams in the library to solicit their feedback on types of activities they would enjoy and feel appreciated by. There were also a number of fond memories of past activities that were collected.

The final result of the task force was a report to library administration that included recommendations on the charge, membership, administration of the committee, budget, additional ideas/potential activities, and an annual recognition event. The recommendations received overwhelming support by administration and were then shared library wide. The Employee Appreciation Committee began its inaugural year in September of 2017.

The membership of the committee is composed of a mixture of faculty librarians and staff as well as a member of the administrative support staff. Members have two-year terms that are staggered so that there are always returning members to maintain continuity. A two-year term also allows members to really invest in the work of the committee during their term and then rotate off for others to have the opportunity to bring their ideas to the group. Each year, a vice-chair is selected to serve as a vice-chair in their first year and then serve as chair the second year. The committee has an annual cycle of July through June with a call for new members each June. After the first year of implementation, where library employees saw what the committee did, the Employee Appreciation Committee was the most requested committee appointment.

Administrative details of the committee involved the decision to meet monthly and that minutes would be taken on a rotating basis by members. Minutes would be available on the library intranet for any library employees to access. The committee would also be sponsored by an associate dean to provide support and guidance to the chair. The task force also outlined an annual budget for the committee. An annual budget allows the committee the flexibility in planning activities and events rather than submitting individually funded event requests. An annual budget for the committee also aids library administration in budget planning and reduces the number of requests throughout the year.

Appreciation Events

The task force recommended that the committee plan at least three events or activities per year in addition to an annual event. Feedback from library employees highlighted the desire to have informal, fun activities, preferably with food. The task force brainstormed ideas with special care given to inclusivity. In the inaugural year of the committee there was a Fall Dessert Competition, support for the annual Library Holiday Brunch, a Chili Cook-Off, and a Summer Games & Ice Cream Party. In addition, an informal recognition board was created. Designated "Belk's Buzzworthy," after the name of our library, the board has blank notes that anyone can fill out to recognize a library colleague. These notes are collected about every other month or if the board gets full! It is wonderful to see all the work being done across teams in the library and colleagues recognizing and thanking each other for outstanding work and kindnesses.

The greatest success of the Employee Appreciation Committee has been the annual recognition event, which was named CeLIBration! This first annual event was held at the end of the spring semester and included all library employees. An upscale lunch was provided and, in recognition of the inaugural event, every library employee received a University Libraries T-shirt. There were games, random drawings for prizes from those recognized on the Belk's Buzzworthy board, and tons of socializing. All of the informal appreciation notes from the Belk's Buzzworthy board were scanned and displayed in rotation on TV screens at the event. Two major awards with nods to our university and location in the mountains were created: Mountain Mover and Appalachian Spirit. A call for nominations was distributed to all library employees and the committee chose the winners who were announced at the event. The winners received a significant technology-related prize and all nominees received a certificate of nomination. The feedback on this event was overwhelmingly positive and ended the academic year with an air of appreciation and collegiality.

Key Considerations

An Employee Appreciation Committee can be scaled to fit any size library organization, however large or small. To get started, propose the idea to someone in your library administration. The support of library administration is crucial as it signals to the organization that morale and team building are important, and that the future committee has their backing and financial support. Next, gather a small group of willing and energetic volunteers to serve as a task force to build your committee. While you might be tempted to jump right in and start planning activities, be sure to develop the parameters of the committee so the structure and work of the committee is clear. The documentation will ensure the sustainability of your efforts.

Key considerations involve the charge, membership, activities, and budget. The task force should write a charge for the committee that clearly outlines what the committee is responsible for and differentiates it from the work of other committees/groups. The charge also helps in recruiting new members. Determine the optimal membership of your committee, including the total number of members so that it isn't too large to work with but has enough members to distribute the workload. Consider the structure of your organization and ensure the committee is representative of all library employees. For example, choose a mixture of faculty and staff or a representative from the various teams within your library. A defined term limit is also suggested as it allows individuals to understand the broad time commitment before volunteering. If your library has an annual process of assigning members to committees, align the Employee Appreciation Committee with this process. Finally, decide who will chair the committee initially and, moving forward, who will choose the chair and members.

Next, get creative and gather ideas for events and activities. There are many ideas readily available by searching the internet or higher education literature. You can also get ideas from your library employees by brainstorming at team or library meetings or by sending out a survey. Also connect with longer-term library employees to learn about past events that went really well or not and why. A variety of events will appeal to your diverse group of library employees and be as inclusive as possible. The timing of events is important to provide the greatest opportunity for everyone to participate. For example, when planning a lunch event, schedule it for longer than just one hour so that those on service desks can more easily attend. If you have second and third shift employees, consider events later in the day that might include them or at times when the library is slower, such as before holiday breaks or the very end of the semester. Even with your best efforts, there are some people who will choose not to participate, and that is their prerogative.

Finally, considering the types of events and activities the committee would like to organize, draft an annual budget. Your library administration may ask you to request funds per event or designate an annual budget which allows the committee more flexibility. Regardless, it is always wise to estimate an annual expenditure for planning purposes. Your library administration may also have to consider which funds can be used on appreciation events for employees. For example, we found that if we purchased gift cards as prizes for our annual event, the recipient would be taxed for them, so we chose to go in a different direction. Understanding any budget limitations upfront will prevent any unnecessary complications with your budget officers.

Finally, the committee should consider how to keep the air of appreciation going year-round. Our informal appreciation notes board is in a highly trafficked area by our mailroom and has encouraged engagement. There is now an electronic version as well. The committee can also consider random acts of kindness such as motivational notes left in mailboxes or positive Post-It Notes on office doors. Many activities can be organized with little or no money! The time and effort of building and running an Employee Appreciation Committee is well worth the result of individuals feeling appreciated and strengthening the connections between library employees.

When YOU Are the Change

Thomas Sneed, *associate professor and director of the law library, Washburn University of Law*

Libraries can experience many different types of changes. The conversation about print and electronic resources has been going on for years. Library spaces are being remade to look more like coffee shops. Long-standing policies regarding food and noise levels are being updated and security devices near entrances are disappearing. In the end, libraries themselves are in a constant state of change.

But what happens when YOU are the change? For two of my three library positions, I have been a major change for the institution. In the first instance, I was hired as a department head after a reorganization of the library structure. Everyone in the library had been reporting to one assistant director and, after my arrival, there were three departments with new reporting structures. In the second instance, I was involved with a major library change with my hiring to replace a retiring director who had been in his position for over 35 years. My arrival signaled major changes for the libraries, and each situation required that certain skills would be needed to successfully navigate the changes.

These two change experiences have significantly affected my library career and my outlook on dealing with change. I have done some things well and also made plenty of mistakes. However, there are three principals I have followed in each situation to support a positive change for everyone involved.

An Open Door Policy (and Remember to Listen)

In both roles, one of the first things I told everyone was that I had an open door policy. If the door was open, which it was the vast majority of the time, everyone was welcome to come in to talk, ask questions, or voice complaints. This sounds easy, but it can be difficult for both sides. Some will be reluctant to speak freely with the person representing the change. It takes time for most to feel comfortable and learn to trust. As the person with the open door, you may feel as if your time is no longer your own. Every stoppage to talk will take away from the work at hand and require additional time to get back on track. However, these conversations will lead to better acceptance of any change. It is not always easy, but the results will be there.

The open door policy can also include a "roaming around the building" aspect. Getting up from our desks is not only healthier, but it can also encourage walking around the library to interact with your colleagues. From a manager's perspective, interacting with colleagues in their office space can also be less intimidating to them and shows you are willing to make the effort to learn about others.

An open door alone is not enough. Listening is a crucial part of the equation. Being a good listener is a skill that can be learned, and then turning conversations into actions completes the circle. This also plays a key role in building trust. The change agent is often someone with whom the remaining staff will not know very well prior to their arrival. Like everything else, building trust will not happen immediately. But if others are willing to take advantage of the opportunity, the discussions will provide insight into each other's thoughts, motivations, expectations, and desired outcomes.

Be an Example (and Own Your Mistakes)

When you are the new person in town, everyone will be trying to figure out who you are. If you are the new leader in town, the employees may be trying to see what they can "get away with." Whatever situation you find yourself in, it will always be beneficial to step right in and get your figurative hands dirty. Find ways to be an example to others and it will be noticed.

What are some librarian duties perfect for providing a strong example? Things like taking shifts at a service point or stacks maintenance duties probably would be high on any list. What would happen if you, as the symbol of change, gladly accepted your fair share of these roles? For each of my two change positions, I have taken on roles that were not expected from the position. In my department head role, I continued to handle reference questions even though my primary role was to delegate the work. We maintained a spreadsheet, and everyone could see that I was taking my portion of the responsibilities and understood the complex questions coming from our faculty. As a library director, I continue to staff our reference desk for at least one shift per week, and I am the volunteer who walks around the building several times per day to facilitate building counts for our statistics. Taking on these small duties is noticed and has allowed me to fit in more quickly with my new colleagues.

Along with setting a positive example, it can also be beneficial to show a willingness to make mistakes. Not all new projects or initiatives are going to work out. Who remembers the buzz from a few year ago over the use of Second Life in libraries? While it never caught on, I am sure the same people who tried Second Life moved on to another new technology, process, or other innovation that has caught on and led to great benefits in their library. Not being afraid to fail leads to innovation and it can also lead to greater acceptance. If your new colleagues see you try new things, with both wins and losses, they may also become more willing to step outside their comfort zones.

Give Credit (and Give Up Your Ego)

If you are in any management position, the notion of giving credit to others is key. This is particularly important for the person who is a symbol of change. There will be a natural impulse to make yourself look good to everyone in the organization as the new person. However, there will be plenty of opportunities to build this good will with others outside the library. The librarians are who you directly work with and you will be best served by showing these colleagues that you both recognize and value their contributions.

There are many situations where others can be given their just due. This can be in emails where their contributions are mentioned, in conversations with other colleagues, and in any other public proclamations. Early on in my time as a manager, one of my employees mentioned that they liked frequent positive feedback. I soon realized this regular positive support made it easier to discuss the problems because everyone also knew when they were doing their work well. This workplace cheerleading had the added effect of allowing more honest conversations about difficult issues.

The ability to give credit to others also leads to a lack of ego. A strong sense of your own abilities may come off to others as arrogance. Confidence that may come across as arrogance is no way to start out in a new position. Deflecting to the work of others is one way to level out any ego that may try to appear. We should all be proud of what we accomplish, but we need to learn to toot our own horns without our egos getting in the way. It is more effective when others talk about your greatness based on your selflessness, work habits, and the work you produce.

Many people are afraid of change. This can be magnified when you are the change occurring in your library. However, having the opportunity to be change should be embraced as a challenge and the organization would not have put you in the position if they did not have confidence in your abilities. By following a few simple rules, such as giving your time, being an example, and leaving your ego at the door, your position as the change agent will invariably be easier than trying to force things along. Change is a constant in all aspects of our lives. Why not do everything in your power to make it positive?

Breaking Out of the Cube (Farm)
Redesigning for Empowerment

Andrea Langhurst Eickholt, *collection management librarian, Eastern Washington University*
Merri Hartse, *discovery services and systems librarian, Eastern Washington University*
Rose Sliger Krause, *metadata librarian, Eastern Washington University*

Sweeping changes in technical services work driven by technology and economic pressures provide opportunities to rethink roles and decision-making in libraries. As staff numbers shrink, and the demand for handling complex tasks rises, it becomes imperative to disrupt the hierarchy and create a more inclusive environment where decision-making is shared. This chapter describes an approach by the Eastern Washington University Libraries' Collection Services unit to empower classified staff in decision-making through a space redesign project, followed by a Plus/Delta evaluation to review positive outcomes and potential actionable improvements.

Technical services units in libraries have undergone tremendous revision in the last 15 years, due largely to economic pressures and technology changes, resulting in fewer staff, less tangible material processing tasks, and an increased focus on collaboration and project work. These changes have shifted the physical space requirements in technical services workspaces from compartmentalized "cube farms," where individuals labored to complete routine manual tasks, to a more complex set of tasks requiring strong communication, problem-solving, analytical, and technical skills (Zhu, 2012). In late 2015, Eastern Washington University (EWU) Libraries' Collection Services unit embarked on a workspace redesign that would more effectively use existing space to meet the needs of changing work tasks and styles. Further, the space redesign project afforded the opportunity to empower paraprofessional staff to become more involved in unit-wide decision-making and outcomes, in order to create a less hierarchical and more inclusive, positive work environment.

EWU is a medium-sized regional comprehensive public university, and the EWU Libraries' Collections Services unit is responsible for all aspects of acquisitions, cataloging, serials, electronic resource management, collection development, and discovery. The unit consists of four paraprofessional or classified staff positions and four professional librarian positions with faculty status. The paraprofessional staff have been with the Libraries for six to 25 years, while all four faculty librarians have been hired in the last one to five years. There is no unit head, the result of intentional flattening of the organizational structure within the Libraries.

Like other academic libraries, the Collection Services unit at EWU has had its staffing level reduced over the last 15 years, especially in lower-level paraprofessional positions tasked with routine clerical work. The unit has witnessed the increase in electronic resource acquisitions and the reduction of print, which has required a shift to a more cyclic, variable, project-based work style, as opposed to the highly structured "linear path of well-defined tasks that are routine and predictable" for physical resource processing (Schmidt and Dulaney, 2014, 69-70). Paraprofessional staff and faculty librarians are also heavily involved in cross-departmental initiatives in scholarly communication, archival collection management, and collection discovery and access. These changes required an updated, flexible workspace that allowed all unit staff to communicate and collaborate, as well as retain the ability to focus on highly complex, technical tasks.

Space for Collaboration

EWU's Collection Services unit is made up of a "self-directed, multi-generational workforce, with employee's expectations of having input in workplace decisions," as well as unit supervisors who use a peer-to-peer management style, rather than a top-down style (vanDuinkerken and Mosley, 2009, 7). The faculty librarians supervising paraprofessional staff hoped to use the space redesign project as a motivational enrichment opportunity wherein paraprofessional staff could have the opportunity to apply their talents, work together to achieve shared outcomes, and perhaps learn new skills in the process (Thomas and Holley, 2012).

Three overarching concepts guided the project:

- Shift to an increasingly project-based and cyclic work environment
- Promote a collaborative work environment
- Empower unit members to make decisions and changes based on experience and expertise

The unit supervisors were particularly focused on using a process that was not faculty librarian-driven, and they acknowledged the experience and expertise of paraprofessional staff in knowing their own work needs and provided them with the opportunity to work collaboratively on the project.

Three paraprofessional staff and one faculty librarian volunteered to serve on the space redesign project team. The initial project meeting in fall 2015 set the stage for group decision-making, individual team member responsibility for specific tasks, and identification of options for moving forward. Tasks identified included an inventory of existing space and furniture, and collection of individual feedback from all unit members during the slow period over the winter holidays. The student worker supervisor focused on outlining specific needs and potential space layout related to materials processing space for student workers. Concurrently, library-wide organizational changes resulted in interlibrary loan functions moving out of Collection Services and into a new Access Services unit. This move, both organizationally and physically, coincided with the Collection Services space reconfiguration process.

Proposal

Using the information collected from unit members, the project team prepared a proposal for library administration that outlined the benefits of space reconfiguration, the consequences of maintaining the current space configuration, the financial support required to proceed with reorganization, and a proposed floor plan. A January 2016 proposal identified benefits and consequences:

BENEFITS
- Lighter, brighter workspace to improve overall atmosphere
- More flexible materials processing space by relocating permanent personnel to the perimeter of the room and consolidating student worker processing space to a centralized area
- Open sightlines to doors and visitors; no one facing away from primary doors (security improvement)

- Decrease the number of small, inefficient workspaces into a centralized area allowing space to be repurposed into a meeting or collaboration space
- Room for flexible project space as needed (positions the unit to be
  more flexible and agile in anticipating future needs)

CONSEQUENCES IF NO CHANGES
- Cluttered work and meeting space (excess furniture and cubicles
  sitting unused in the center of the room)
- Disorganized, non-defined workspaces
- Inefficient student worker processing spaces scattered around room
- Blocked sightlines from safety/security standpoint
- Underutilized space

Implementation

Library administration approved implementation of initial and low-impact
(i.e., low-cost) changes in late February, and facilities staff began to dismantle and remove furniture no longer needed. The space included about four
cubicles (with furniture) that were vacant due to staff reductions, as well as a
plethora of wall-mounted bookshelves not needed as acquisitions continued
to shift away from print to electronic. Workflow efficiencies were gained by
moving a CD/DVD disc cleaner to Circulation so that discs could be cleaned
at the point of return rather than shuffling those items back and forth to
Collection Services. Utilizing desk-high cubicle walls available through the
university's surplus furniture supply allowed creation of more open materials
processing areas. Two of the four paraprofessional staff also self-elected to
use three-foot high cubicle walls in order to increase sightlines and improve
face-to-face communication, which increased the collaborative atmosphere
of these workspaces. Library administration financially supported the costs
of the reconfiguration: approximately $3,600 to university facilities for fur-
niture reconfiguration and minor repairs and electrical work, and $4,200 for
shorter cubicle walls for staff workspaces. A final round of surplus furniture
removal was completed in May 2016. Towards the end of 2016, the Collection Services unit celebrated the reorganized space with an open house for all
library employees. Collection Services showcased the newly organized space,
with special emphasis given to the collaborative work of the project team to

improve the overall space. The open house was an opportunity to internally acknowledge the teamwork of project members, as well as the contributions of all unit staff.

Results

A few months after settling into the newly redesigned space, concerns surfaced regarding unanticipated outcomes of the project, specifically increased noise. In response, unit supervisors chose to utilize a Plus/Delta evaluation model. This model had been successfully used by previous library leadership as an opportunity for individuals to provide feedback experiences on projects or events with a focus on improvements through action, rather than outlining negatives alone. In the Plus/Delta model, plusses were positive aspects and deltas were areas for improvement. A goal of the space redesign evaluation was to intentionally focus on the positive outcomes of the redesigned space and identify *actionable* future improvements. At the start of the evaluation discussion, participants were reminded that improvements should be specific, action oriented (begin with a verb), and within the realm of possibility. A staff member from outside the Collection Services unit facilitated the Plus/Delta session to provide a neutral perspective and to inspire a discussion in which all voices could contribute observations and concerns. The question identified in advance to help direct the discussion was "How do our observations impact the work of the unit?" This question guided the conversation beyond personal preferences and unanticipated disadvantages, to actionable changes that would support unit functions. Staff identified several positive aspects of the space redesign, as well as several actions that could ameliorate increased noise in the reconfigured space.

PLUSSES (POSITIVE ASPECTS OF THE CHANGE)
- More functional workspaces, more desk space, more spacious
- Less cluttered, less junk
- More room for meetings and teambuilding (also known as snacks)
- More inviting with better visibility
- More interactive

DELTAS (ACTIONS FOR IMPROVEMENT)
- Experiment with white noise devices (mitigate noise from side conversations and printers)

- Make headsets available to those that don't already have them
- Invite visitors into office spaces to reduce distraction in main work-space (increase awareness of noise levels, extended conversations, with professional responses for distractions)
- Investigate sound absorption solutions and potential for ceiling-height partitions

Focusing the Plus/Delta discussion on actionable improvements further reinforced the space redesign project's goal of empowering paraprofessional staff to make decisions and changes to improve unit functions. All unit staff were encouraged to request headsets through the library's administrative office, with the goal of using headsets to both block out noise and use when listening to webinars. This low-cost solution allowed individuals to control sound concerns themselves at their point-of-need. Other noise control improvements, such as a white noise machine, were tested but did not gain traction, while financial constraints limited the implementation of sound absorbing devices and ceiling-height partitions.

Since the workspace redesign, the Collection Services unit has further increased its collaborative and project-based work. For example, ongoing changes and annual maintenance of the library's proxy server shifted from one faculty librarian position outside Collection Services to a shared undertaking by two classified staff and one faculty librarian within Collection Services. All three staff collaborate in troubleshooting and making file stanza changes throughout the year. This shift has allowed for more seamless electronic resources management, as well as encouraging teamwork as a means of success. With the increase in collaborative work, the unit continues to grapple with increased noise levels in the space. The open, inviting atmosphere of the space has encouraged unit staff to interact more with each other, and library staff outside the unit regularly enter the space to consult Collection Services staff on a project or initiative. While the resulting increased noise level can be distracting at times, the welcoming collegial atmosphere is well worth the potential loss of productivity.

EWU Libraries' Collection Services successfully redesigned its workspace to be more inviting, encourage collaboration, and function to support changed requirements for less physical processing and fewer staff. The redesign project was used to engage paraprofessional staff in the process of making changes, rather than handing down pre-determined edicts from faculty librarians. The Plus/Delta evaluation method provided the mechanism for action-oriented improvement, rather than negative litanies. It is hoped that this more open atmosphere encourages positive communication and interaction, resulting in both higher staff morale as well as the potential for innovation resulting from the free exchange of ideas.

References

Schmidt, K. & Dulaney, C. K. (2014). From print to online: Revamping technical services with centralized and distributed workflow models. *Serials Librarian, 66*(1-4), 65-75.

Thomas, J. R. & Holley, R. P. (2012). Management versus repetitive tasks - avoiding "working for the weekend": A crash course in motivating library staff faced with seemingly endless tasks. *New Library World, 113*(9/10), 462-473.

vanDuinkerken, W. & Mosley, P. A. (2009). Increasing investment through participation: Redoing workspace layouts without tears and angst. *Library Leadership & Management, 23*(1), 5-11.

Zhu, L. (2012). The role of paraprofessionals in technical services in academic libraries. *Library Resources & Technical Services, 56*(3), 127-154.

Making the Implicit Explicit
Whiteness, Conflict, and Power in a Library Mentoring

Steve Whitley, *clinical assistant professor, University of Illinois at Chicago*

Program Context

I am currently a clinical assistant professor in the University Library at the University of Illinois at Chicago, and, up until very recently, was the only member of the faculty who was not a degreed librarian. I have an M.Ed. and oversee and teach in the Intergroup Dialogue Initiative, which joined the University Library in 2014. (Intergroup Dialogue has been widely practiced and researched by institutions and scholars for several decades. For a comprehensive review, see Gurin, Nagda, and Zuñiga, 2013.) In the summer of 2017, I was approached by my dean about assisting in improving the library's mentoring program because of my training and experience in facilitating difficult conversations, especially about race. At that time, I knew I would soon be assigned a mentor, which made for an intriguing opportunity because of how paradoxical it seemed; I am not a librarian, my colleagues' work greatly differs from mine, and I am not an experienced mentor. Over the next few weeks, I was able to identify a few different issues by separately meeting with mentors, mentees, and department heads. This chapter will focus on one of those issues and how we have used dialogue to begin addressing it: the often unnamed, unstated, and consciously avoided conflict that resides in conversations about diversity, specifically among white people.

Over the course of the 2017-2018 academic year, the mentors and I met nearly monthly to investigate whiteness. For this work I was awarded the

Dean's Special Award of Merit in the spring of 2018, which had not existed prior to my work with the mentors. In our meetings, we were also able to begin forming relationships with one another where experiences and emotions are acknowledged and validated, and mistakes can be instructive. Through dialogue, we have been able to explore cultural values that are facets and products of white culture, especially in higher education, such as: meritocracy and individual production; the expectation of comfort; sociocultural power; and the assumption of objectivity. In a field where individual achievement and merit are valued most and determine promotion and advancement, here was an opportunity to critique the circumstances that only facilitate success for some.

It is not my intent to minimize the contributions from the people of color present for these conversations, nor to render them invisible. Rather, it is to emphasize the importance of white people learning to understand the power and influence we hold. It is to also highlight that one reason I am even writing about this is because I am a white man talking about race. Because of my race and gender, my credibility is often assumed.

Identifying Conflicts

The mentors are all faculty at the associate or full professor level, all MLIS-degreed librarians, 90 percent of them are white, and all have seniority and administrative power. Mentees are mostly MLIS-degreed faculty at the assistant level, with greater racial diversity, who do not have seniority or administrative power. While mentors quietly acknowledged the racial dynamics present, they did not seem to have the vocabulary to talk about it with one another. Further, the relational foundation of the mentoring program was understood to be functional rather than personal. In this, guidance provided by mentors focused on their mentee's productivity.

Most of the conflict was not between individuals or even with the program's existence. Rather, it was buried in the assumptions and rules of professionalism that are often racialized, gendered, and classed. The rules are largely unwritten but specific, dictating the ways we navigate power, conflict, comfort, and emotions. Mentors generally felt secure when bringing up conflict as it related to unmet expectations, goals, or agreements, especially pertaining to research and writing projects. These are professional issues they had navigated before, could speak to with authority, share their experiences about, and exert power given to them by the organization. However, there was uncertainty and unawareness when it came to personal and/or sensitive issues, such as race, culture, or un(der)valued labor. They struggled not only to identify, validate, or challenge issues that arose, but to cultivate relationships where those discussions could take place. Inversely, mentees often felt compelled to assure their mentors of their competence, thereby minimizing the personal, professional, and cultural insecurities they experienced. All of this was known, but not named or discussed.

The Dialogic Framework

Central to a dialogue's success is the participants' willingness to explore issues of identity (race, gender, sexual orientation, dis/ability, etc.) and their connections to sociocultural power. These can be difficult topics, and dialogue requires us to move beyond stating an opinion to speaking from experience (or lack thereof). Our framework prioritizes a process that fosters empathy, perspective-taking, and trust as foundations for having sensitive conversations and working toward social change. Guiding this process are facilitators trained to identify and name conflict, manage interactions, emotions, and participation, and navigate the interpersonal and historical power dynamics of those involved. A key motto in dialogue is "to make the implicit explicit," because naming something allows us to start dealing with it directly. This can be as "simple" as identifying and attempting to normalize the tension we feel with one another, or as complex as naming the ways gender, race, and socio-economic status inform how we communicate and interact. We challenge participants to seek connections with one another amid conflict and to seek understanding with one another, even if they disagree with what the other person is saying. This is not easy work for anyone.

As a dialogue educator, I understand that before many sensitive topics can be broached, a relationship characterized by trust, mutual respect, and ongoing consent must exist. These conditions take time to develop and are essential for these exchanges to be valuable. In the library, mentor-mentee relationships were more often assigned than naturally developed and mutually chosen. There are no supervisor-employee mentorships, but the relationship is nevertheless one in which the mentor holds organizational power and the mentee does not. Our experiences follow us to (and happen at) work and personal, sensitive issues often arise. Those conversations often involve risk and vulnerability, especially when there are power differentials regarding one's place in the organizational hierarchy or broader social standing. People often do not feel equipped to discuss these topics and are generally motivated to preserve their relationships. All of this affects the way in which conflict is approached and navigated (or avoided).

Breaking the Silence

In my first meeting with the mentors, I was introduced as being there to "talk about diversity and mentoring" with them. Instead, I requested that we talk about whiteness because 1) 90 percent of the people there were white, 2) discussions about race frequently and unfairly burden people of color with educating white people on how racism works, and 3) white people are more open to hearing about racial issues from another white person (a phenomenon known as the "white speaker effect," coined by writer Chauncey DeVega). In that moment, I felt the air leave the room. Everybody shifted. Naming what was present but had gone unnoticed made it real, which produced conflict. By processing what happened to us all in that moment, we were able to find common ground in the awkwardness. We were able to normalize the discomfort, defensiveness, and fear that happens when we are reminded of, or told about, our whiteness. After that was normalized, we were able to talk about what prompted those reactions. Some people mentioned feeling guilty; others mentioned not having the words to talk about being white. This has been the starting point for our mentors, and for many white people beginning a journey of racial consciousness: getting past the initial emotional distress of speaking the unspoken. We have neither developed a vocabulary to talk about being white nor learned to navigate the emotions produced when asked to look at our racial history. Our silence prevents opportunities to find and name root causes, and to investigate and learn about their effects. Because of our instinctive guilt, we tend to prioritize the temporary discomfort we feel rather than consider the historical oppression of others.

The Language of Diversity vs. White Supremacy

As mentioned, the mentors are overwhelmingly white, and this is often the case at other institutions. While efforts have been made to diversify the faculty, simply hiring librarians of color for faculty positions does not guarantee their inclusion, retention, or advancement. A common issue is that of the "well-meaning white person," one whose personal politics and conscious beliefs embrace equity or inclusion, but whose actions or unconscious attitudes may harm the people and communities we want to support. We can extend this to our institutions, who champion diversity through increased efforts to recruit and hire faculty of color but wonder why they are not retained after their (often invisible) labor is dismissed or devalued. White supremacy affords us the privilege, as white people, to individualize the issues rather than looking at the system itself. While individually we may not be racists, we do exist in a racist culture and at times unintentionally reproduce the beliefs, norms, and values of it.

I want to pause to clarify something here: by using the term white supremacy, I am not specifically referencing the KKK or racist individuals. I am, however, naming a comprehensive system of racialized protection, power, and control for us and systemic oppression and violence for others. I want to be explicit, too, about implicating us—white people—in its maintenance; every system requires ongoing practices. White people have a vested interest in maintaining this system and challenging it is difficult. Using the term white supremacy decenters individual consciousness and intent, and instead describes one aspect of the United States at a cultural level. If language and culture have a cyclical relationship, new language may be needed (Gramsci, 1971).

One of the most impactful sessions with the mentors was about how the language we use influences how we think and behave. By unpacking terms like "cultural competence," "ethnic," "multiculturalism," and "diversity," we explored the ambiguity of their definitions. More importantly, we came to understand that we apply those responsibilities to others while exempting ourselves. Those words maintain our racial comfort and they give our institutions moral credibility. (Robin DiAngelo's *White Fragility* is an excellent starting point for a thorough review of these concepts.)

In their ambiguity, those terms create a binary of "racist" and "not racist." Reframing the way we talk about and engage with these issues can be powerful. By refocusing our attention on histories, institutions, norms, and belief systems that were created and have always been controlled by white people (Lipsitz, 2006), the power of white culture becomes the starting point for analysis. This can have important implications for both policy and culture.

Opting In

As of August 2018, the mentors have dedicated roughly 15 hours to this process. In July of 2018, we shared racial testimonies, which are the stories of our lives through a racial lens. Because this experience is new to them, their racial journey was entered through an aspect that was much more accessible to them—being targeted by another form of oppression (e.g., the impact of being working class, a woman, LGBTQIA+, and/or having a disability, etc.). But knowing that there is now a group of white people who have participated in this exercise in our library, who are willing and able to have these types of conversations, is encouraging. Not only have they started developing a consciousness about their whiteness, but they have also begun developing a vocabulary to talk about it, and the confidence to do so. Imagine what is possible with 50 hours. With 100 hours. With 1,000 hours.

Prior to beginning my work with the mentoring program, mentors rarely convened to talk about their practice, to share stories of success or frustration, or to reflect on the intents and goals of the program. They tended to focus on the work required for promotion and advancement without considering the broader context in which it occurs or the forces contributing to it. I want to acknowledge that the mentors have approached this work with courage and curiosity and have committed to this process. They did not have to do any of this, and for that I am impressed and grateful. My colleagues should be applauded for their willingness to be critically reflective of themselves and longstanding practices. The fact is, they are challenging themselves to do more.

References

DiAngelo, Robin (2018). *White fragility: Why it's so hard for white people to talk about racism*. Boston, MA: Beacon Press.

Gramsci, Antonio (1971). *Letters from prison*. New York, NY: HarperCollins. (Gramsci expresses the power of language to establish boundaries of what can be communicated. Also consider various shifts in language, such as the development of taboos in using slurs for people of color, queer people, people with disabilities, etc., and subsequent attempts to reclaim said words.)

Gurin, Patricia, Biren A. Nagda, & Ximena Zuñiga (2013). *Dialogue across difference: Practice, theory, and research on Intergroup Dialogue*. New York, NY: Russell Sage Foundation.

Lipsitz, George (2006). *The possessive investment in whiteness: How white people profit from identity politics*. Philadelphia, PA: Temple University Press.

Identifying and Confronting Bullying

Alice Eng, *electronic resources librarian, Wake Forest University*

I have been part of the workforce for more than 20 years. In those two decades, I have worked in various fields, but my most recent work experience is as a librarian. Almost every employer for whom I have worked has required me to attend seminars, workshops, or discussions about appropriate workplace behavior. After participating in these trainings multiple times at various jobs at different organizations, I was more than confident I knew the meaning of bullying. I was sure I knew how to identify a bully and bullying. In the examples shown to me by employers, a bully was aggressive in some way: maybe verbal, maybe physical, but always recognizably aggressive. A bully was also always angry. Bullies yelled, were condescending and insulting. They also violated personal space. Those were supposed to be the all-encompassing telltale signs of a bully bullying.

Bullying does not always resemble the examples employers and the media give us. A person who does not yell, is not hostile, is not physically aggressive, nor acts belligerently can still be a bully. I would guess that many people who have been or are bullied have experiences that do not mirror the videos they have seen from HR departments. Nor do their experiences match the extreme cases we know from movies, television, and the media. The villains in those stories are easy to identify. Bullying in the workplace can be more nuanced and harder to recognize. It can be more psychological and passive-aggressive. Identifying bullying may be even more difficult when you are the target of a bully.

The Difference Between Harassment and Bullying

Bullying and harassment are often used synonymously but only harassment is legally defined. Bullying is up to the interpretation of individual institutions. According to the U.S. Equal Employment Opportunity Commission (EEOC), harassment is "unwelcome conduct that is based on race, color, religion, sex (including pregnancy), national origin, age (40 or older), disability or genetic information." Harassment applies to the treatment of a class of defined groups of people. Harassment can be a form of bullying and is illegal. Most employers currently view bullying as unethical behavior only. There are no such protections or legal definitions for bullying, which makes it harder to prove.

There are many resources that can help you understand bullying better. The Workplace Bullying Institute (WBI) conducts research on bullying. Their website defines workplace bullying as "repeated, health-harming mistreatment of one or more persons (the targets) by one or more perpetrators. It is abusive conduct that is:

- Threatening, humiliating, or intimidating, or
- Work interference—sabotage—which prevents work from getting done, or
- Verbal abuse."

The literature about bullying and libraries provides other helpful definitions for workplace bullying. One example is Bonnie A. Osif's article, "Workplace Bullying." It defines workplace bullying as "behavior that threatens, intimidates, humiliates, or isolates people at work, or undermines their reputation or job performance."

Bullies likely do not see themselves as bullies and will even less likely see fault in their behaviors. Bullies may be acting unconsciously. Bullying behavior might be explained by the perpetrator as being perfectionists, having a "Type A" personality, acting on behalf of the organization, or offering constructive criticism.

The Targets

Despite our assumptions of who we think are likely to be targeted, people who are targeted are not typically weak, strange, or socially awkward. Research shows the exact opposite. According to the WBI, targets are people who are sociable, skilled, work well with others, and independent.

Are You Being Targeted?

Though research about bullying in libraries is limited, the literature that does exist provides good examples of bullying. The broader research about bullying and academia also provides a good framework for understanding acts of bullying. As mentioned before, the WBI's website lists examples and definitions of bullying in the workplace. Literature focusing on workplace bullying consistently states that many people who are targeted are unaware that they are or were targets. Many do not realize they were bullied until they read examples of others' accounts.

Bullying takes many forms and can happen in any part of your work life. Bullying may be focused on harming your job performance. Examples include

- being excluded from projects that directly correlate to your job;
- supervisor(s) giving poor evaluation with no prior meetings about performance;
- evaluations that nitpick your job performance;
- supervisor(s) refusing to assist and respond to issues you have articulated as difficult or problematic;
- supervisor(s) withholding information that directly impacts your performance;
- being assigned tasks that specifically highlight perceived weaknesses.
- supervisor(s) delaying or denying things that all other employees are entitled to (timely evaluations, travel reimbursement, formalized/ regular meetings);
- supervisor(s) monitoring your conversations;
- supervisor(s) referencing your personhood or character and inappropriately correlating it to job performance (accusations such as lacking loyalty, clouded judgement, displaced empathy, and internalizing processes are blamed for poor job performance); and
- supervisor(s) retaliating against you for not accepting the blame for bad decisions and policies (phrases like "throwing under the bus," or "shifting blame," might be used).

Another form of bullying is social isolation. Social isolation harms emotional well-being. Examples include

- being told that the organization is not for everyone (meaning, *you*, specifically);
- supervisor(s) not speaking to you or acknowledging you (the "freeze-out");
- supervisor(s) refusing to advocate for you;
- coworkers telling you what "others" think about you and your job performance without solicitation;
- comments about what makes you "different" than others in the organization;
- coworkers informing you that you should not expect others to accept you;
- being forced to explain yourself and your actions in front of a group when no one else is required to do the same;
- coworkers and/or supervisor(s) creating, participating, and condoning a hostile mob environment (*we* think you are inappropriate; *we* agree that you are mistaken);
- meetings that are purposely structured to be adversarial and you are outnumbered or have no advocate; and
- provocation in group settings, usually through passive-aggressive remarks.

Bullying can happen when someone infringes upon your physical workspace. This harms your ability to feel in control of your own personal space. Examples include

- uninvited and unannounced coworkers disrupting your work and work area,
- coworkers monitoring your conversations—interjecting themselves into conversations you are having with other people, and
- you have made obvious attempts to disengage or distance yourself from interacting with harmful coworkers who continue to corner you in your work area.

Confronting a Bully

If you decide to stay in your position and confront bullying, this list of suggestions may provide some assistance and relief. A warning: you may have to repeat your story many times and you may have to escalate your problems to library directors or deans, or outside your library. You should be prepared for possible dead ends, meaning some people will tell you they cannot or will not do anything.

- Document EVERYTHING. This cannot be stressed enough. Because bullying is based on the repetition of offensive behavior, make sure to record details of the incidents, the dates, and how you reacted. Workplace bullying takes place over an amount of time. It can be difficult to recall exact dates and situations several days, weeks, or months after they have happened. Additionally, you should document any meetings you have with management, administration, workplace advocacy groups, and human resources. Documentation is a powerful tool when presenting your case to decision makers.
- Contact your Employee Assistance Program office. These offices offer counseling or can match you with counselors who specialize in workplace bullying. A counselor can help you cope with workplace stress, anxiety, and depression as well as give you advice about how to handle bullies. Counseling is often covered by your insurance plan.
- If you can, find a coworker you trust. A coworker who has worked at an organization for an established amount of time can tell you about other instances of bullying that may have occurred. It is unlikely you are the first person who has been targeted by the bully. If you can establish a pattern of bullying, it is easier to force your management, administration, or human resources to act.
- You do not have to disclose your story to anyone who you feel will question you. The "devil's advocate" is a common position for many people when presented with a narrative. However, your emotional well-being is the priority and having to explain and prove your experience can make you question yourself and feel worse. Surround yourself with people who know you well enough to provide you with positive support and do not require you to defend yourself.
- Talk to your HR department. This can be a difficult step for many reasons. HR departments have reputations for protecting the interests

of an institution and not the employee. However, it is important that you make them aware of the situation. Make sure that all meetings are documented (who you met, when you met, topics covered).

• Talk to your union or local staff/faculty advocacy group. Not all schools have unions, but they may have something equivalent, such as the American Association of University Professors. These groups can help you understand your rights, your contract, policies, and more. Also make sure your conversations are confidential.

• Schedule a meeting or regular meetings with your supervisor(s). If a coworker is bullying you, speak to your supervisor. A good supervisor will listen to you and be responsive. He or she will intervene, find a way to limit communication, or remove you from the situation. If the bully is your supervisor, you may need to meet with your department head or the dean or director of your library. Many times, deans and directors are unaware of what is happening in departments and rely on department heads for information, which is one-sided. Your director or dean needs to hear your side of what has occurred to make a fair decision. Again, it also forces administration to be accountable. You may be able to request a representative from human resources, your union, or advocacy group to be present at these meetings. Though they may not be able to speak on your behalf, they can be present to take notes or mediate.

Conclusion

This chapter is not about overcoming bullying. That implies you can defeat the emotional damage and impact of bullying. For most, that is not the reality. This chapter is about coping with a traumatic event and attempting to gain control of your emotional well-being and workspace, lessening the need to look over your shoulder and feeling less victimized. There is no data regarding the number of targets who have found success confronting their bullies. This is likely due to a scarcity of research about bullying and libraries, and targets underreporting their experiences. The literature that does exist about bullying and libraries indicates that bullying is not uncommon. Nor is it uncommon for targets to be unable to identify that they are being bullied. From personal experience, the suggestions I listed were successful; however, they may not work for everyone. Someone's best option may be to leave their position.

Every situation and person are different and there is no right answer. If you have reached a level of despair that is negatively impacting your work or your mental health, I hope the suggestions above offer you some path forward.

References

Harassment. (n.d.). Retrieved August 22, 2018, from https://www.eeoc.gov/laws/types/harassment.cfm

Osif, B. A. (2010). Manager's bookshelf: Workplace bullying. *Library Leadership & Management*, 24(4), 206–212. https://journals.tdl.org/llm/index.php/llm/article/view/1859/1132

Workplace Bullying Institute - WBI - help, education, research. (n.d.). Retrieved August 22, 2018, from https://www.workplacebullying.org/

Recommended Reading

Bartlett, J. (2016). Workplace bullying: A silent epidemic. *Library Leadership & Management*, 31(1), 1–4. Retrieved from https://uknowledge.uky.edu/libraries_facpub/278

Freedman, S., and Vrevin, D. (2016). Workplace incivility and bullying in the library: Perception or reality? *College & Research Libraries*, 77(6), 727-748. https://doi.org/10.5860/crl.77.6.16553

Motin, S. H. (2009). Bullying or mobbing: Is it happening in your academic library? *Library Faculty Publications*, 28. http://repository.stcloudstate.edu/lrs_facpubs/28

Ryan, M. (2016). Management: Besting the workplace bully. *Reference & User Services Quarterly*, 55(4), 267–269. http://dx.doi.org/10.5860/rusq.55n4.267

Staninger, S. W. (2016). The Psychodynamics of bullying in libraries. *Library Leadership & Management*, 30(4), 1-5. Retrieved from https://journals.tdl.org/llm/index.php/llm/article/view/7170

Diversity Training for Culturally Competent Library Workers

Madeline Ruggerio, *librarian, Queensborough Community College SUNY*

D iversity training would provide strategies for creating practical tools that allow staff and librarians to develop an open and flexible approach to patrons while maintaining a welcoming climate for the library work force and students. Training would allow staff to move campuses forward in terms of fulfilling their goals for multiculturalism and diversity. Cross-cultural communication skills, cultural sensitivity, and effective listening skills are the *sine qua non* of effectively serving a diverse community. Training would allow librarians and staff to examine their own cultural backgrounds and increase their awareness of personal values, assumptions, and biases. Librarians have been predominantly white, and the field of librarianship is slow to diversify to reflect the communities they serve. In 2006, the American Library Association released a comprehensive study called "Diversity Counts" to demonstrate the need to recruit a diverse workforce in the field of librarianship. The most recent report, released in 2012, shows that there has only been a 1 percent increase in nearly a decade of racial and ethnic minorities working as credentialed librarians—from 11 percent in 2000 to 12 percent in 2009-2010. I worked for a state college in an affluent New Jersey town whose student body was made up of mainly upper-middle-class white youth. My well-accomplished colleague, who was pursuing a PhD at the time, was working at the reference desk one evening when a student asked, in a dispassionate manner, to speak with the librarian for some research help. The student assumed the highly educated African American female sitting behind the reference desk was not the librarian.

Library employees need to be taught how to understand the patron's reactions and perspective from the inside. A way to respond to and acknowledge cultural difference is to offer staff training sessions to ensure positive interactions with patrons. While libraries strive for equitable services, each library user has a different need. Students vary in terms of educational backgrounds, financial support, language abilities, and cultural perspectives. Building an environment that is inclusive and engaging for foreign students is important. Libraries can use training sessions to gain insight and understanding into policies and procedures, and into how to improve them to meet the needs of a diverse population. The intention of the training session would be to make personnel aware of cultural and linguistic differences. Workshops can be designed to help staff feel what one might experience when traveling to a new culture and encountering different values, customs, and social interactions. A training session would make staff aware of how to communicate with library users who are new to American libraries. Because the system may seem complex and difficult to navigate, the same quality service to one group can be extended to other groups with customized changes. We have a legal obligation to provide service without discrimination based on race, gender, sexuality, religion, physical disabilities or cultural differences. When serving a diverse population, varying perspectives of opinions and books need to be included in the services delivered by staff and librarians. Another major concern among education libraries—and one that goes hand in hand with diversity—is inclusivity. Inclusive library services, where many perspectives are offered to a diverse population, is important. It is important for a variety of population views not to be excluded. Library employees need to be aware and knowledgeable of inclusive services to a diverse population.

Training would highlight unintentional and intentional processes of racism, classism, homophobia, and sexism. Therefore, understanding and learning about the many facets of diversity needs to be a priority for staff and librarians. We need to be taught about the multiple aspects of diversity, including race, ethnicity, gender, sexuality, economic conditions, physical ability, and recently migrated populations. We need to acknowledge the existence of other group identities related to culture, ethnicity, social class, gender, and sexual orientation. Are we as professionals prepared to provide customized quality service to the increasingly diverse populations that frequent our libraries? On the job training is essential to prepare us to deliver quality, equitable service to diverse populations. We do not approach patrons with a one-size-fits-all mentality. Each request requires a different approach, even if the patrons are asking the same question. It is our job to provide customized service to meet the needs of groups and individuals who use the library. We need to learn how to recognize and respond to the newly emigrated patron whose behavior is unique to a specific group. The process of effectively and compassionately helping diverse communities involves an awareness and knowledge of the population that makes up the community. We as staff and librarians need to learn how to be culturally competent in our jobs and in our relationships with our coworkers. The ALA is a proponent of promoting training opportunities for library personnel to provide effective service to diverse populations. Library professionals need to get to know their community, so they can tailor services to their specific information needs.

When interacting with patrons, library professionals should be sensitive to cultural differences, language barriers, and accents. How can staff and librarians best serve adult learners with physical disabilities, cultural and social differences, gender identities and sexual orientations, and non-English speaking and developmentally delayed adults? Community colleges cater to nontraditional students of varying degrees of academic ability. The goal of libraries is equitable service to all populations with customized services when required. We must offer equal access to information. Training could offer a foundation on which to build empathy and cultural competence, offering employees the opportunity to adjust their attitudes and behavior as they develop an understanding of the cultural belief systems of patrons and see and appreciate the variety of humans around the world. Instructional strategies on how to communicate with people of a different culture or race would foster respectful interactions with patrons and lead to effective service.

At one time, foreign students studying in the United States were predominantly from European countries, where the economy, language, and culture are similar to the United States' economy, language, and culture. Today, more students come from Asia, India, and other developing countries. Cultural backgrounds of these diverse groups can differ from the mainstream culture in their use of libraries. These differences include religion, communication, dress, and world views influenced by native homeland customs. Trainees' knowledge of religious beliefs and practices could make for a smooth interaction with the Muslim student who may use a quiet, seemingly secluded section of the library to place his prayer rug and perform one of his required 5 daily prayers. Design thinking can be used to create a space that would meet the needs of this community. The design thinking process would require input from the staff and community. A survey or questionnaire could be given to students and staff on how and where to best implement a quiet open space. This could generate many creative ideas as solutions.

Staff and librarians need to be aware of the need to speak slowly, clearly, and with no use of idioms or jargon when communicating with students who have had limited exposure to the English language. Since communication skills vary among students, library workers need to be sensitive to the soft-spoken, timid student who is not confident speaking English. We should be made aware of other viewpoints and preferences, such as the religiously conservative male student who is more comfortable speaking with and taking directions from a male rather than a female. Knowledge of this approach bias regarding gender in this cultural community would ease communication and interactions in the library. Staff also need to be sensitive to a male who has always used the restroom as a coed facility in his native village and has never been exposed to gender-specific restrooms. Training would prepare the library staff to communicate effectively with the students and exhibit patience. Cross-cultural understanding could encourage the employee to be flexible and understanding, allowing the patron, in the ideal scenario, to communicate how much culture has to do with his decision to walk into any restroom, regardless of gender. This cultural misunderstanding is a result of his adjustment to new living conditions with new cultural rules. In this case, a friendly explanation of the use of separate restrooms would suffice, rather than an admonishment and calling security.

If we treat our patrons with respect and empathy, they will continue to frequent the library. We must be taught the range of issues these diverse populations face and how to provide services that meet their expectations in order to adequately serve them. All librarians and staff need to be taught how to be culturally competent. We need to show an interest to understanding the needs of the transgender population. Libraries can support LGBTQ and transgender colleagues by working towards creating an accepting and welcoming work environment for LGBTQ and transgender library staff. Gender-neutral, single-stall restrooms, where a key does not need to be requested, and with signage that is representative of all genders, will create a safe space for this population. An established remote process for name changes, without the need for legal identification, should be made available such as via email or fax. The removal of titles such as Miss/Ms. or Mr. on library forms and communications would also help the transgender population feel less anxiety. As a collection development librarian at CUNY, I include a substantial amount of recent LGBTQ material in the form of fiction and nonfiction. The common read that most community colleges participate in should include an LGBTQ novel one year with planned events and displays highlighting the novel.

Training will give the employee the ability to monitor their own adjustment to a new culture. Diversity training can prepare staff and librarians for how to deal effectively with diverse populations. We need to make staff aware of the social and cultural differences that exist in our community. We need to go beyond cultural awareness and take action by training library personnel to be respectful and empathic through continued learning about the cultures, customs, behaviors, and information needs of the community. What do those who are members of the Muslim faith require from us as information specialists? We need to recognize, understand, and implement measures that meet the needs of their communities. For example, Muslim women wearing headscarves or burkas should not have to worry about being physically or verbally accosted for doing so.

Discussions of shared experiences in a training session could highlight situations we may encounter in our daily interactions with our patrons. By examining and identifying underlying issues of oppression and personal bias that produce inequality in diverse communities, personnel would acquire a skill set to ameliorate unpleasant interactions. Training programs should include a discussion of beliefs and biases associated with specific populations and train staff on how to communicate effectively. Diversity training can help raise awareness of one's own possible hidden biases. Guiding trainees to identify and examine their own patterns of unintentional and intentional racism, classism, and homophobia is essential. Self-reflection on one's own cultural background often leads to acceptance of others. Acknowledging suppressed stereotypes and perspectives towards others would facilitate respect for others. Training can lead to positive attitudes among employees to diverse patrons. Program planners use group discussions, personal journals, situational role playing of cultural groups, and feedback to create self-awareness among trainees. Strategies could be developed to better serve patrons from other cultures. Training sessions would provide the ability to communicate, interact, negotiate, and intervene on behalf of clients from diverse backgrounds. The culturally competent librarian can conduct self-assessment and is aware of how his or her own values, biases, attitudes, and beliefs may affect different or minority patrons. The culturally competent librarian can incorporate his or her values and knowledge into aspects of policymaking, administration, practice, and service delivery. Guidelines need to be discussed and implemented on how to treat this emerging culture so that all libraries can become inclusive and fulfill the goals stated in their mission statements.

Creating Spaces for Culture Conversations
Developing a Webinar Series

Jewel Davis, *education librarian, Appalachian State University*

T
he North Carolina Library Association (NCLA) is an organization devoted to supporting the library community by providing professional development, informing members about library legislation, publishing library research, and awarding scholarships. Similar to national and state library associations, NCLA has a variety of sections that promote the interests of its members. The Roundtable for Ethnic Minority Concerns (REMCo) is a committee that strives to serve as a voice for ethnic minority members. REMCo provides members with opportunities to network, discuss, and learn about the various issues faced by underrepresented ethnic minority librarians and the services library workers can provide to diverse library populations.

In 2016, the chair of REMCo proposed a new online initiative, Culture Conversations with REMCo, to address current issues faced by diverse library workers and promote positive and critical discussion in and around the library workplace. Outside of digital newsletters and email communications, REMCo had primarily provided opportunities for member engagement through paid face-to-face events. While the REMCo events were well attended and garnered positive feedback, REMCo leadership was interested in creating a free online space for discussion and learning. This initiative would also help bridge the time gaps between semester-based events and continue our conversations in accessible formats through which many more members and interested library workers could participate.

The REMCo executive board developed the initiative as a webinar series in which invited scholars and leading experts presented to participants for 30-40 minutes and then participated in a moderated Q&A discussion portion. From 2016-2018, we hosted webinars featuring ethnic minority librarians, scholars, and business professionals on the following topics:

- Race and the Professional Workplace
- Libraries and Social Justice
- Imposter Syndrome
- Diversity, Cultural Competence, and Power in LIS
- Building Diverse Collections for K-12 students
- Microaggressions in the Workplace
- African American Genealogy
- Creating Inclusive Organizations
- Workplace Identity and Deauthentication

In total we have had over 1,000 registrants, 450 live participants, and 1,000 webinar recording views. These participants came from across the United States and consisted of LIS students, library workers, and non-library university departments. The series has received positive feedback and has not only impacted REMCo members locally but has also connected our members to advocates and allies around the United States. Due to this success, REMCo plans to continue hosting and archiving the series. What follows are steps REMCo took in developing the webinar series and tips to consider if you want to create a similar initiative. The "Webinar Resources" section at the end of this chapter provides a list of popular webinar tools and archived webinars from REMCo and NCLA.

Choosing a Webinar Platform

There are a number of free and paid webinar systems available. When choosing a webinar platform, consider the following questions to help you determine the types of features the webinar system should provide:

- What is your budget for a webinar system?
- How many live attendees do you expect, and how many can the webinar system accommodate?
- Do you want the system to provide a registration form and automatic emails to participants?

- What interactive features (chat, polling, breakout rooms, video and audio, etc.) do you want speakers and attendees to have access to?
- Do you want the system to record and archive the webinar session?

We chose to use the paid subscription-based Zoom webinar system because it can support up to 500 participants (depending on the subscription level), has automated registration, offers session recording, and provides a variety of interactive tools speakers and attendees can use during the webinar.

Platform tip: Many institutions and organizations already subscribe to webinar conferencing systems, so a member of your committee or group may already have access to one. Consider reaching out to your members to see if a system may be available for your use.

Selecting Webinar Topics

We took a few approaches in selecting topics and speakers for the series. When we first began the series, we researched and discussed current trends and issues around diversity in librarianship and identified speakers who were conducting research in the areas of social justice and racial inequality in the workplace.

After hosting two speakers on these topics, we felt REMCo members had a sense of what the series was about, so we then surveyed our members for topics they felt represented the challenges they were facing in the profession. This led to us finding speakers for webinars that addressed issues of imposter syndrome, cultural competence, and microaggressions. We also gave REMCo members the opportunity to speak in the series by sharing their own areas of research and library work. REMCo members presented webinars on African American genealogy and diverse youth literature.

By this point, we had successfully conducted a number of webinars and were getting attendees and interest from people outside of NCLA and REMCo, and we felt it was important to extend our call to participate and present to librarians of color across the United States. We sent a call for presentations through We Here (librarieswehere.wordpress.com), a supportive collaboration and mentor social media network created specifically for librarians, archivists, and library and information science students of color. We Here has open and closed social media platforms, and we sent our wider call through the closed platforms. Members of the We Here network presented in our series on inclusive organizations and racial identity.

We found all of these outreach approaches to be helpful in creating a dynamic webinar series that represented current trends, member issues and expertise, and affiliate interest and expertise. We intend to continue using the above approaches in choosing future topics and speakers for the series.

Topic tip: Outside of surveying your members for topics of interest, consider browsing ALA's Center for the Future of Libraries Trends website. The site highlights and provides resources on a variety of relevant trends in libraries and librarianship.

Soliciting Webinar Speakers

If you plan to reach out to a speaker you have identified, be sure to first consider compensation. If your group has the funds to provide an honorarium, do so, and be upfront about compensation when sending the initial query. While webinars do not require travel, it is important to acknowledge the time a speaker gives in preparing and delivering a presentation. If your group has a limited budget, consider low-cost ways to show your appreciation, such as providing free or discounted group membership or waiving the fee for a future professional development you host. If you can't provide compensation, sending a small gift or token to a speaker after the presentation can go a long way in showing your appreciation.

No matter the type of compensation or gift, always send a formal letter of appreciation after the session expressing your gratitude for the speaker's contribution and impact. For speakers in academia, letters can be used as support for promotion and tenure. For other speakers, these letters can be included in personnel files and used to show their impact in the profession.

When we solicit speakers, we also highlight who we are as an organization, the reasons we specifically reached out to the individual, the impact we think they could have on our members, and the ways in which we can support them through advertising and providing a platform for them to reach our members and interested affiliates around the United States.

Speaker tip: Look for experts in your local community who may be willing to offer their time at no to little cost in order to promote their work and network with others in the community. Providing opportunities to build community locally through making local connections can enrich the relationships and partnerships between your organization and your community.

Webinar Advertising

To advertise our series, we use a combination of listservs, social media platforms, and personalized emails. When we advertise, we also include a link to our past archived sessions, which helps give new participants an idea of what to expect, and it continues the promoting of past sessions.

If you have a potential audience or group in mind, intentionally focus on the social spaces these members frequent and consider sending more personalized invitations. If you know established and trusted members within the target audience, reach out to them to help promote your session. Promoting beyond the traditional listserv invites will show potential attendees you are willing to make an effort to outreach more intentionally.

Advertising tip: When seeking larger audiences, think about what other disciplines outside of librarianship may be interested in the topic. Participants and speakers from outside of our field can bring a valuable diverse perspective to the conversation.

Additional Tips to Consider

Below are a few additional tips to keep in mind that we have found to be helpful.

1. Offer your speaker time before the session to practice and/or familiarize themselves with the webinar system. Taking the extra time to ensure the speaker is comfortable will help the webinar run more smoothly.
2. If you will be hosting many webinars, consider purchasing headphones with an integrated microphone to help ensure high audio quality.
3. Be sure to obtain permission from the speaker to record the session and be mindful of sensitive issues addressed among participants during the session. If the speaker or participants do not want names or other specific information shared, redact accordingly in the audio or chat log.
4. If you want to include participants in different time zones, be mindful of the webinar time. A mid-day webinar allows for people on both sides of the US to participate at a reasonable hour.
5. If possible, set up your webinar session to automatically record. Getting everyone settled into a webinar and starting on time with intro-

ductions and moderating can be a lot to do at the beginning. You can easily forget to hit record!

Creating the Culture Conversations with REMCo webinar series has a been a positive experience for our members and has created additional avenues for connecting with people interested in addressing and discussing issues that matter to our members. The success of the series has encouraged us to continue providing free online opportunities for our members and interested affiliates to gather together, learn about important issues, and have conservations that push us forward into positive change.

Webinar Resources

NCLA WEBINARS

- College & University Section
    - » Archived webinars: http://www.nclaonline.org/college-university
    - » Virtual conference webinars: http://www.nclaonline.org/college
      -university/event/save-date-cus-one-day-virtual-conference
- Distance Learning Section
    - » Webinar Wednesday archives: http://www.nclaonline.org/dls
- Help! I'm an Accidental Government Information Librarian Webinars
    - » YouTube channel: https://www.youtube.com/channel/UC6Cfuale
      U8N77us06prY10Q
- STEM Librarianship in NC
    - » YouTube channel: https://www.youtube.com/channel/UCZvq
      HAXfObtg7WPxevf-eCQ
- Roundtable for Ethnic Minority Concerns
    - » Archived webinars: https://sites.google.com/view/remco
      webinars/past-webinars
    - » YouTube channel: https://www.youtube.com/channel/
      UCAbK7V6XDYTguM2L9gWiBMw
- Technology & Trends Section
    - » YouTube channel: https://www.youtube.com/channel/
      UC51Eq-yruaBwafxWwRWFo9Q

POPULAR WEBINAR PLATFORMS

- Adobe Connect: https://www.adobe.com/products/adobeconnect.html
- Google Hangouts: https://hangouts.google.com/
- GoToWebinar: https://www.gotomeeting.com
- Skype: https://www.skype.com/en/
- WebEx: https://www.webex.com/
- Zoom: https://zoom.us/webinar

ABOUT THE EDITORS AND CONTRIBUTORS

Editors

HEATHER SEIBERT is currently employed by National Heritage Academies in Winterville, NC. Before her current position, she was employed at East Carolina University in the Department of Research and Scholarly Communications. She holds a Masters in Library Science from ECU and is currently pursuing her Doctorate of Education in Curriculum and Instruction from the University of North Carolina Wilmington. She is an advocate for work-life balance, women's rights, and lactation compliance in the workplace. Her research interests concern open educational resources, Creative Commons Licensing, and affordable textbook creation in higher education for support of K-12 curriculum and instruction.

AMANDA VINOGRADOV works for East Carolina University's Joyner Library in the Special Collections Cataloging department. She holds a Masters in Library and Information Science from the University of North Carolina at Chapel Hill. Her research interests include digital libraries, public health, and community outreach.

AMANDA H. MCLELLAN is the assistant director of discovery and technology services at East Carolina University's Joyner Library, and adjunct lecturer at the University of Illinois School of Information Sciences. She holds her MLIS from the University of Illinois at Urbana-Champaign, a BA from DePauw University, and is currently pursuing her Doctorate of Education with a focus in Higher Education Administration. Her research interests include library technology, usability and user experience, and library management. A member of the Greenville Noon Rotary Club, Amanda enjoys giving back to the community, baking, and spending time with her husband, dog, and cats.

159

Contributors

ANTHONY AMODEO retired in 2015 after a nearly 40-year career working at a private research library, a state university library, and a private university library, in positions from research assistant in rare books to instruction coordinator to associate librarian for reference and instruction. He co-authored a library science textbook and has contributed articles and chapters to library-related publications.

KELSEY BRETT is the head of discovery and metadata department at the University of Colorado, Denver, Auraria Library. She received her Master of Science in Information Studies from the University of Texas School of Information.

ALEX BYRNE is a youth services librarian with the Pierce County Library System, stationed at University Place, WA. When not helping people with their technology issues or telling stories to young children and their parents in fleece pajamas, they are extolling the virtues of library cards, promoting off-the-beaten-path books to readers, and trying to understand their communities more.

DONNA E. COGHILL has focused her career in education, instruction, and outreach. Currently, the community engagement librarian and coordinator for campus partnerships, she provides research and teaching services for service-learning courses, as well as outreach support for living learning programs. Currently on campus, Donna is a VCU Green Zone volunteer, a facilitator for the VCU Safe Zone program, a member of Equality VCU, and serves on the VCU Police Department's LGBTQ+ Safety Advisory Group, including co-facilitating Trans Sensitivity in Policing workshops.

MELODY CONDRON is the resource description and management coordinator at the University of Houston Libraries, where she manages materials cataloging and record quality control projects. She holds an MLS from the University of North Texas and a BA in Communications and Media Studies from Penn State, Behrend College.

JEWEL DAVIS is the 2017–2019 chair of the North Carolina Library Association's Roundtable for Ethnic Minority Concerns. She is an education librarian in a PreK–12 Curriculum Materials Center at Appalachian State University's

Belk Library and Information Commons. She works with education and LIS students, youth librarians, and teachers on using diverse youth literature, incorporating STEM and emerging technologies into classroom practice, and developing practitioner-based research skills. She received an MA in teaching from the University of North Carolina at Chapel Hill and an MLIS from the University of North Carolina at Greensboro.

ELIZABETH DILL is the director of library services and assistant professor at Troy University in Dothan. She holds an MFA from CalArts and MLIS from Valdosta State University. She is currently a doctoral student at Valdosta State.

M. TERESA DOHERTY is assistant head for information services, and a teaching and learning librarian, at VCU Libraries. She has participated as a member of the ALA Intellectual Freedom Committee for many years and the experience has informed her research interests, which include access, equity, and privacy (and the Oxford comma). Teresa is a jack-of-all-trades in library outreach, assisting researchers on the desk, through chat/text/email services, library instruction, and social media.

PATRICIA M. DRAGON is the head of special collections cataloging at East Carolina University and has been practicing yoga for 25 years. She is a founding member of the Joyner Yogis.

SUSAN ECHOLS is a library assistant for technical services at Troy University's Dothan campus library. She holds a BS in Finance and a MBA, both from Troy.

ALICE ENG is the electronic resources librarian at Wake Forest University. She has worked as a librarian at different institutions for almost ten years. Before working in libraries, she worked in television.

MERRI HARTSE is the discovery services and systems librarian at Eastern Washington University. Previously, she served in management, access services, and systems-related positions spanning academic, public, and law libraries.

KAYLA KUNI is a librarian for Pasco-Hernando State College (FL). She earned her MLIS in 2014 from the University of South Florida (USF), Tampa. She is currently working on her MBA at USF.

ANDREA LANGHURST EICKHOLT has worked at Eastern Washington University since 2015, currently as collection management librarian. Before coming to EWU, she worked in a variety of roles at the University of Notre Dame and as a corporate technical services librarian in upstate New York.

LISA MARTIN is the coordinator of outreach at the University of Houston Libraries, where she leads a team focused on liaison engagement to the campus and community. She received her MLIS from the University of California at Los Angeles and her BA from the University of Redlands.

MAGGIE MASON SMITH received her MLIS from the University of South Carolina, Columbia, in 2012. She currently works as a library specialist in the Resource Sharing unit of Clemson University's R.M. Cooper Library and has over eight years' experience in a variety of roles within Access Services. She devotes many service hours to diversity initiatives on Clemson's campus each semester, and she is excited to work on LGBTQ+ initiatives and toward a greater recognition of Indigenous culture on campus in the year to come.

RACHEL M. MINKIN is currently head of reference services at Michigan State University (East Lansing, MI). Rachel has also served as an information literacy librarian at MSU, as a reference and instruction librarian at Lansing Community College (Lansing, MI), and as a reference librarian at the Graduate Theological Union's Flora Lamson Hewlett Library (Berkeley, CA). Rachel's earned her MLIS at University of Pittsburgh and also holds a Master of Theological Studies (MTS) from Vanderbilt Divinity School (Nashville, TN).

TASHIA MUNSON is an access services and outreach librarian at the University of Michigan. Her research interests include services for traditionally underrepresented students in higher education, distance learning, and intentional leadership principles. She received her MLIS from Wayne State University in 2013.

JENNIFER NATALE has an MLIS from Rutgers University, MS in Counseling from Springfield College and BS in Psychology from the University of Connecticut. She has a background in academic librarianship, student development, and nonprofit administration. She is currently a liaison librarian at Appalachian State University's Belk Library and Information Commons.

MEAGHAN O'RIORDAN is the accessioning and collections manager at the Stuart A. Rose Manuscript, Archives, and Rare Books Library at Emory University, where she manages the receipt, accessioning, and initial processing of rare book, manuscript, and archival material. She received a MS from the University of North Carolina at Chapel Hill in 2014. Meaghan has served as chair of Emory University's Library and IT Services' Wellness Committee since March 2018.

MADELINE RUGGERIO is an academic librarian at Queensborough Community College CUNY. She is a first-generation Italian American and has watched the struggles her immigrant parents have endured.

EMILY SCHARF is head of reference and instruction at Laurence McKinley Gould Library at Carleton College in Northfield, Minnesota. Prior to this position, she was an instruction and liaison services librarian, then head of research services at Webster University in St. Louis, Missouri. She has an MA in Library and Information Studies from the University of Wisconsin-Madison and an MA in Nonprofit Leadership from Webster University.

ROSE SLIGER KRAUSE is metadata librarian at Eastern Washington University. She previously served as curator of special collections at the Northwest Museum of Arts & Culture/Eastern Washington State Historical Society.

ANGEL SLOSS is a digital reference and embedded librarian for Tennessee State University. She previously worked as a learning resource center manager for a for-profit college and as a teacher librarian for the public school system in Tennessee.

THOMAS SNEED has his BA in History from the University of Evansville, a JD from the University of Kentucky College of Law, an MLIS from Kent State University, and an MBA from Emory University Goizueta Business School. His areas of research and teaching interests include research pedagogical issues and leadership/management in both the library and legal contexts.

REBECCA TATTERSON is the electronic resources librarian at East Carolina University and has been practicing yoga since taking a class in 2005. She is a founding member of Joyner Yogis.

REBECCA TOLLEY is a professor and librarian at East Tennessee State University. She coordinates the Sherrod Library's research consultation service. She speaks and publishes on topics such as organizational culture, the digital divide, and social media. She co-edited *Generation XLibrarian: Essays on Leadership, Technology, Pop Culture, Social Responsibility and Professional Iden-*

tity (2011) and *Mentoring in Librarianship: Essays on Working with Adults and Students to Further the Profession* (2011). Her writing has appeared in anthologies, several library journals, and numerous reference works.

STEPHANIE VAN NESS earned her Master of Arts in Information Resources and Library Science from the University of Arizona in 2013. She has worked at Northern Arizona University's Cline Library since 2008. In addition to libraries in general, Stephanie's interests include student employment, user experience, and equitable employment practices.=

HEIDI VIX is head of resources management services at Webster University. She received her BS from Hanover College and MLS from Indiana University with a specialization in Technology Management. In her previous role as an electronic resources librarian, she presented at local and national conferences on negotiating with vendors.

DOROTHY WAUGH is a digital archivist at the Stuart A. Rose Manuscript, Archives, and Rare Book Library at Emory University, where she is responsible for the acquisition and management of the Rose Library's born-digital collections. She received a MLS from Indiana University in 2012 and a MA in English Literature from the Ohio State University in 2010. Dorothy served as chair of Emory University's Library and IT Services' Wellness Committee from August 2017–March 2018.

KATY WEBB is the head of research and instructional services at East Carolina University and has been practicing yoga since taking it as an elective in graduate school. She is a founding member of the Joyner Yogis.

STEVE WHITLEY administers and facilitates courses in the Dialogue Initiative at the University of Illinois at Chicago in his role as a faculty member of the University Library. Most of his work is in building spaces with students to explore issues related to identity, sociocultural power, and oppression. This is done through a process designed to build empathy, understand differences, and use conflict as a tool for learning.